USA RVers

Road Atlas 2025

Hit the Road Smarter in 2025 – Discover Scenic Routes, Hidden Gems, and Expert Navigation Tips for the Ultimate RV Adventure Across America

Cassandra M Joseph

DISCLAIMER

All trademarks, service marks, and trade names referenced in this travel Atlas belong solely to their respective owners. The author and publisher make no claims to ownership or endorsement and are not in any way affiliated with them, and any use of trademarked material is exclusively for informative purposes and reasons.

TABLE OF CONTENTS

MAP OF USA
Map With QR Code
INTRODUCTION
Welcome to the Ultimate RV Road Atlas
What's New in 2025
How to Use This Atlas Effectively
Chapter 1: RV Road Travel Essentials
Choosing the Right RV
Packing Smart for the Road
Safety Tips & Emergency Prep
RV Etiquette & Campground Rules
Chapter 2: Planning the Perfect RV Trip
Route Planning Basics
Boondocking vs. Campgrounds
Budgeting for Fuel, Campsites & More
Seasonal Travel Tips
Accessibility & Pet-Friendly Travel
Chapter 3: Scenic Byways & Iconic Routes
Pacific Coast Highway (CA to WA)
Route 66 (IL to CA)
Blue Ridge Parkway (VA to NC)
Great River Road (MN to LA)
The Loneliest Road (US-50)
Alaska Highway (Dawson Creek to Fairbanks)

DISCLAIMER
USA RV SCENIC ROUTES

Chapter 4: Regional RV Adventures

Northeast:

New England Fall Foliage Loop
Adirondacks & Finger Lakes
Coastal Maine Route
Southeast:
Great Smoky Mountains Explorer
Florida Keys RV Escape
Bluegrass & Bourbon Trail
Midwest:
Lake Michigan Circle Tour
Badlands & Black Hills Trek
Ozarks Scenic Drive
Southwest:
Grand Circle National Parks
Route 66 Highlights
Texas Hill Country Adventure
West:
California Coast & Wine Country
Yellowstone to Glacier Loop
Oregon & Washington Cascades
Northwest & Alaska:
Olympic Peninsula Journey
Idaho Hot Springs Trail
Alaska Marine Highway & Interior
Chapter 5: RV-Friendly National Parks
Top 20 RV-Accessible National Parks
Reservation Tips & Park Regulations
Navigating Narrow Roads & Height Limits
Chapter 6: Hidden Gems Off the Beaten Path
Underrated State Parks

Small Town America with Big Charm

Unique Festivals & Local Eats

Chapter 7: Campground & RV Park Directory

Top-Rated Campgrounds by Region

Hookup Availability & Amenities

Booking Resources & Membership Clubs

Chapter 8: Maps & Route Overviews

State-by-State RV Road Maps

Fuel Station & Dump Site Locator

Public vs. Private Parks

USA RV SCENIC ROUTES

MAP OF USA

Map With QR Code

SCAN THE QR CODE

INTRODUCTION

Introduction: Welcome to the Open Road 2025.

The buzz of your RV motor as it rumbles to life, the vast open road extending eternally before you, and the exhilaration of not knowing what hidden surprise awaits you just around the corner are all indisputably amazing. Whether you're a seasoned road warrior or just starting out on your first major trip, the journey is always more exciting when you have the correct guide—and USA RVers

Road Atlas 2025 is the perfect co-pilot.

This is not your typical road atlas.

This book is designed for dreamers, doers, and full-throttle wanderers. Inside, you'll discover thorough, full-color maps of every state in the United States, as well as skillfully chosen itineraries tailored exclusively to RVers. From winding mountain passes in Colorado to breezy coastal roadways in Florida, from desert hideaways in Arizona to wooded byways in Oregon, you'll discover some of America's most gorgeous, quiet, and breathtaking routes.

But we did not stop there. This handbook is full with rare information, including:

Hidden gems and lesser-known places will not be found in regular travel guides.

Expert suggestions for RV travel, including road grades, height clearances, and fuel stops.

Recommended RV parks, boondocking areas, and campsites, with honest observations about facilities and accessibility.

Seasonal planning ideas to help you decide when (and when not) to travel

Custom route suggestions for weekend trips, full-time RVers, and everything in between

Bonus: Easy access to offline and online interactive maps to keep you on track, even when your Wi-Fi fails.

Whether you're planning a cross-country journey or chasing sunsets state by state, this book will give you the confidence to go farther, wiser, and stress-free. With each page flip, you are not only navigating roads, but also uncovering amazing memories one mile at a time.

So fuel up, turn on your GPS (and maybe a song or two), and let US RVers Road Atlas 2025 take you through a year of unforgettable adventures.

The road is beckoning. Are you prepared to answer?

Welcome to the Ultimate RV Road Atlas

Welcome to the USA RVers Road Atlas 2025, your important tool for navigating the vast and diverse landscapes of the United States with accuracy, confidence, and adventure in mind. Designed exclusively for RV travelers, this atlas combines essential topographical detail with handpicked travel insights to turn the trip into a destination in and of itself.

This book, which spans from coast to coast, provides a detailed look at the greatest routes, RV-friendly services, and beautiful treasures that characterize the American road trip. Whether you're planning a seasonal migration, visiting national parks, or seeking small-town charm off the main road, this map provides the clarity, coverage, and context RVers want.

What makes this Atlas unique?

This is more than simply a map book; it is a fully integrated planning system designed for travel. Every page is tailored to RV-specific requirements, including clearance heights, slope warnings, campsite proximity, fuel station access, and service stops. From Class A motor coaches to camper vans, the information is current, dependable, and simple to use.

Each geographic part combines detailed cartography with road-tested trip information. Scenic byways are marked, and alternative routes are recommended for worthwhile excursions. Icons indicate must-see locations, dump stations, overnight parking, BLM property, rest sites, and RV repair facilities, making it easy to make choices on the road without retracing or guessing.

Navigate with confidence.
This atlas divides the continental United States into manageable travel zones based on state and area. Every map has these features:

Routes that are clearly labeled for RV use include major highways, interstates, scenic byways, and minor roads.

Essential Services: Diesel fuel stations, LP gas refill stations, RV mechanics, and approved service facilities.

Campground Indexing: Contact information and accessibility data are cross-referenced for public, private, and boondocking campgrounds.

Terrain Awareness: Elevation profiles, steep slopes, switchback alerts, and mountain pass recommendations assist drivers anticipate obstacles.

Weather considerations include climate zones, storm-prone places, and seasonal travel recommendations for effective preparation.

Beyond the road: enriching the journey.
In addition to the maps, there is a comprehensive directory of experiences created for travelers who consider the road as more than just a means of transportation—it is a portal to exploration. This handbook contains:

Top 100 RV Scenic Drives: Selected for their natural beauty, cultural relevance, and driveability.

The Hidden Gems Index features lesser-known sights, eccentric roadside Americana, and crowd-free natural treasures.

State highlights include historical routes, Native American territories, national monuments, and regional festivals.

Park Access Planning: RV-friendly approaches to all 63 national parks, including site-specific parking, size limits, and reservation techniques.

Urban RVing Tips: Learn where to park, how to avoid congested areas, and which cities allow overnight stays.

Smart Planning Features

The rear of the atlas contains vital charts and quick-reference aids for safe, efficient travel.

RV Maintenance Checklist

Fuel Cost Estimator and Mileage Tracker.

Dump Station Locator by State

Travel Time Calculator

Towing and Weight Limits Reference Guide

State-by-State Vehicle and RV Regulations

How To Use This Atlas

Use it before your trip to plan a memorable itinerary. Use it while driving to avoid traps and turn with confidence. Use it at night, while stopped under desert stars or seaside pines, to plan the following step with clarity and joy. Whether you're full-time, weekends, or snowbirding, this atlas is your guide.

It's more than simply getting from point A to point B; it's about making each mile count. With the USA RVers Road Atlas 2025, the road isn't only open. It is optimized.

Let the engine hum. The map is in your hands. The path awaits.

What's New in 2025

The open road is evolving—and by 2025, RVers will see a landscape distinguished by new options, enhanced infrastructure, and technologies customized to life on wheels. Whether you're planning a cross-country trip or a weekend loop, knowing what's new this year will help you plan better, simplify your travels, and enjoy every mile of the route.

Expanded National Park Reservation System

Over 30 renowned national parks, including Arches, Glacier, Rocky Mountain, and Yosemite, now demand timed access or vehicle reservations during busy seasons. The National Park Service's 2025 implementation will feature increased digital booking choices via the Recreation.gov app, as well as GPS notifications for admission windows and real-time status updates. Plan months in advance for high-traffic locations, and consider midweek entry to minimize capacity constraints. Parks such as Zion and Acadia have also implemented special RV-only scenic slots on shuttle systems, an innovation intended at reducing congestion in gateway regions.

Electric RV Charging Corridors.

With the advent of electric and hybrid RVs, 2025 marks a key milestone: over 12,000 miles of US roads now have Level 3 DC Fast Charging stations that are particularly designed for RV dimensions and turning radius. Fast-charge hubs are situated every 100 miles along key arteries such as I-10, I-40, and I-95. Tesla's new Supercharger V5 network, which works with adapters for other EV RVs, now takes third-party bookings via its mobile app. Campgrounds along these roads are increasingly offering dual electric and potable water connections, as well as solar-powered charging stations in isolated boondocking regions.

State-Level Infrastructure Upgrades
Several states have undertaken significant developments intended with RV travel in mind:

Texas has introduced 42 additional full-hookup pull-through sites to state parks in the Hill Country Trail and Pineywoods districts.

Montana has extended shoulders and improved slopes on US Route 2 to better handle heavy trucks in Glacier Country.

Florida has created a test program along the A1A Coastal Scenic Byway, which combines storm-resistant RV sites with environmentally friendly garbage facilities.

Highway signs, rest station facilities, and overnight parking possibilities are now more RV-friendly than ever before, particularly in areas where nomadic movement has increased since 2020.

Boondocking Has Gone Mainstream

Public land agencies, notably the Bureau of Land Management (BLM) and the United States Forest Service, will use new geotagging rules in 2025 to assist RVers in locating scattered campsites while safeguarding environmentally sensitive zones. Many formerly informal locations have recently been professionally recognized, with specific pads and stay limitations. Look for the new Leave No Trace Preferred label in mobile applications and maps, which indicates sites with correct gray water disposal access, solar potential, and low-impact zones.

Smart Navigation with RV-Specific Routing

The 2025 generation of navigation systems is designed particularly for RV size, bridge clearance, propane limits, and terrain adaptability. Garmin, Rand McNally, and CoPilot have all upgraded their devices and applications to include AI-enhanced detour forecasts and route flexibility based on real-time weather, roadwork, and car diagnostics. Expect fewer erroneous turns and more efficient fuel stops, particularly with data from truck stop networks such as Love's and Pilot Flying J.

Campground booking evolves.

Gone are the days of uncertain supply. The most recent iteration of campground management systems—used by KOA, Thousand Trails, and independent parks—includes interactive site selection with 360° views, confirmed vehicle fit, and RV category filtering. A new alliance of public and private campsites has recently established the StayReady platform, which syncs last-minute cancellations, waitlist

warnings, and reward points across over 5,000 facilities nationwide. Expect more competition for high-demand sites, but improved tools to help you manage the process.

Real-time Weather and Fire Alerts

Increased wildfire danger, high rainfall, and wind events continue to affect many locations in the West and South. In response, NOAA and FEMA collaborated to create an RVer Alert Grid, which is now incorporated into various GPS systems and weather applications. This system sends route-specific information based on RV-friendly detour access, fuel availability, and overnight shelter appropriateness during severe weather. Particularly useful for travelers going through California, Arizona, Oregon, and the Gulf States.

In 2025, four new National Scenic Byways will be approved for RV adventure.

Missouri's Ozark Highlands Byway winds through wooded hills and limestone bluffs, with renovated turnouts.

The Great Basin Frontier Trail in Nevada highlights distant desert history while providing additional BLM access points.

Georgia's Coastal Colonial Corridor is suitable for leisurely travel through historic villages and barrier islands.

Idaho's Clearwater Loops include improved signs, pull-offs, and interpretive panels for RV-friendly exploring.

These developments provide less-traveled alternatives to busy corridors, which are great for tourists seeking both peace and landscape.

Cross-border Travel Enhancements

Both Canada and Mexico have improved RV border crossings by implementing new pre-clearance and digital customs applications. To lower RV wait times in 2025, major ports of entry (particularly Sweetgrass, Montana and San Ysidro, California) have extended lanes and modified inspection methods. Mexico's RV Permit Express system now accepts vehicle import documents and insurance validation completely online, which is a nice change for winter snowbirds coming south.

As the road ahead unfolds, 2025 marks the maturing of RV travel—from rustic adventure to high-tech ease. This year's upgrades are more than just keeping up with a growing community; they're intended to make RVing more accessible, efficient, and rewarding than ever. Turn the page, set your sights on new horizons, and head into the future with assurance.

How to Use This Atlas Effectively

This road map is designed with the RV traveler in mind—it's clear, intuitive, and packed with useful resources to make your trip a pleasant, enjoyable adventure. Whether you're a full-time RVer, a seasonal traveler, or a weekend adventurer, the style of this atlas offers rapid access to important information while minimizing clutter. Here's how to traverse the sites with accuracy and confidence.

1. Understand the Layout: Region by Region and State by State.

The atlas is organized into six main regions: northeast, southeast, Midwest, southwest, west, and Pacific Northwest/Alaska. Each area has a state-by-state analysis, which begins with a full-page overview map for easy orienting. This is followed by comprehensive state maps, which emphasize

Main roads and RV-friendly routes

Scenic byways and lesser-known alternatives

Camping and RV parks (public and private)

Fuel and propane station markings

Elevation changes and grade warnings for steep passes

Area overview pages serve as jumping-off points for long-haul planning for multi-state road journeys, allowing you to stitch together smooth, efficient routes without neglecting area attractions.

2. Icons and Symbols: The Language of Road

Understanding the visual shorthand of this atlas is critical for quick decision-making when on the go. Key symbols used throughout are:

▲ Campground options include national parks, state parks, and private sites.

❖❖❖ RV Service Centers: Repair, maintenance, and dump stations.

⛽ Fuel stops provide gasoline, diesel, and propane.

🏔 Scenic stops include viewpoints, significant sites, and must-see diversions.

■ Overnight parking at rest areas, Walmarts, and truck stops.

● Compass points indicate elevation and direction change.

Each map has a legend designed specifically for RV navigation, as well as bigger type and high-contrast colors for easy reading in broad sunshine or dark cabin lighting.

3. Trip Planning Resources: Mileage Charts, Elevation Guides, and Weather Zones

At the beginning of each state portion, you'll discover a Mileage Matrix with significant city-to-city distances—a handy reference for calculating fuel stops and driving hours. Elevation profiles for mountain routes are offered to assist you prepare for engine strain, braking risks, and weather changes.

Color-coded weather bands indicate seasonal road conditions—snow-prone passes, hurricane zones, or flood-prone areas—allowing you to arrange diversions or layovers appropriately. QR codes inserted at the bottom of selected pages provide real-time weather and road status information.

4. Hidden Gems & Scenic Routes: Pages with the ☀ emblem recommend worthwhile excursions, including historic villages, odd roadside sites, and hidden parks for RVers seeking quiet or local flair. These carefully picked side roads have been approved for RV access (length and height clearance have been checked), and they feature turnaround alternatives for bigger rigs.

You'll also see "Top Scenic Loops" highlighted in bold lines—multi-day itineraries developed exclusively for RVs, along with suggested overnight breaks, important sights, and typical travel durations.

5. RV-Specific Safety and Accessibility Tips
Margin notes throughout the atlas give crucial travel recommendations geared for RV travel:

Bridge clearance notices in both urban and rural locations.

Tips for navigating steep hills and tight roadways.

Notes on road surfaces and unpaved stretches

Turn radius issues for Class A, B, and C RVs

Where applicable, pages provide toll road information and whether RVs are allowed or prohibited, particularly in tunnel zones or mountain parkways.

6. Cross-Reference Tools and Indexing
A detailed index at the rear of the atlas contains the following:

City and town lists

National and state park names

Campground indexes include page references.

Major scenic byways and road designations

There's also a Quick Trip Planner grid for major RV destinations, which will help you get from Yosemite to Zion, the Great Smoky Mountains to the Florida Keys, and dozens of stops in between.

7. Bonus Resources

Monthly Travel Calendar: Ideas for where to go each month based on weather, crowds, and events.

State-specific RV laws include overnight parking rules, maximum RV speed limits, and towing regulations.

RV maintenance logs and checklists: These pages, located at the rear, allow you to monitor service history, tire rotations, fluid changes, and seasonal preparation activities.

Using this atlas as your navigation co-pilot will not only save you money on diversions and obstacles, but it will also reveal the visual richness, cultural oddities, and huge natural variety that characterize the American road. Every map is more than just a road; it's a strategy, a safety net, and an encouragement to explore more intelligently. Keep it within reach, and the wide road will do the rest.

Chapter 1: RV Road Travel Essentials

Choosing the Right RV

Choosing the correct recreational vehicle (RV) is an important first step toward a safe and fun road trip. With so many models and features on the market, the procedure needs a strategic strategy that balances vehicle capabilities with travel objectives, lifestyle choices, and budget. This section offers a clear, structured framework for travelers to make educated decisions before hitting the road.

Classification of RVs

RVs are generally classified into two types: motorized (motorhomes) and towable (trailers and fifth wheels). Each has its own set of benefits and limits.

Motorhomes

Class A motorhomes

Size: 26 to 45 feet

Class A RVs, which are built on heavy-duty bus or commercial truck chassis, provide high-end luxury, ample living space, and extensive onboard amenities.

Ideal for full-time RVers, extended family trips, or those who value comfort and convenience above mobility.

Considerations include worse fuel efficiency, restricted access to smaller campsites, and more upfront and maintenance expenditures.

Class B campervans.

Size: 17 to 23 ft.

Class B RVs are tiny and nimble, resembling high-roof vans. They often feature sleeping quarters, a small kitchen, and a wet bathroom.

Ideal for: Solo travelers or couples looking for a simple, fuel-efficient travel alternative.

Considerations: Limited storage, small living space, not ideal for long-term living.

Class C motorhomes

Size: 20 to 33 feet

Overview: Class C versions, which are built on a truck or van chassis, include a cab-over berth and combine Class A luxury with Class B maneuverability.

Ideal for: Families or groups that want adaptability, enough room, and simpler handling than Class A vehicles.

Considerations: Less roomy than Class A; gas economy may vary depending on weight and topography.

Towable Units

Travel Trailers

Size: 12–35 feet.

Travel trailers are the most adaptable and diverse RV category, since they can be towed by a variety of cars with correct hitching.

Ideal for: Anyone with a competent tow vehicle and a desire for versatile camping choices.

Considerations: Hitching is required; fuel economy is dependent on the towing vehicle; and backing up might be difficult for novices.

Fifth Wheel Trailers

Size: 25 to 45 feet

Overview: These trailers are designed with a raised front portion and a fifth-wheel hitch attached in the bed of a pickup truck, providing great room and stability.

Ideal for: Long-term travelers that want extensive storage, home-style comforts, and safe towing.

Considerations: Requires a heavy-duty vehicle; not recommended for individuals without prior expertise pulling hefty weights.

Pop-up Campers and Teardrops

Size: 8 to 16 feet (collapsed).

Overview: These lightweight, compact units expand to expose sleeping and culinary rooms.

Ideal for weekend explorers, national park campers, and those with minimal storage or towing capacity.

Considerations: Limited insulation and features; not appropriate for all-weather or full-time usage.

Matching RV Types and Travel Styles

Weekend Warriors: Focus on mobility, simplicity of setup, and cost-effectiveness. Class B vehicles and compact travel trailers do well here.

Full-time explorers need long-term comfort, storage, and trustworthy systems. Class A RVs and fifth wheels are excellent possibilities.

Family Vacationers: Space and sleeping capacity are important. Class C motorhomes and mid-sized travel trailers provide a decent balance.

Boondockers and Off-grid Adventurers: Look for self-contained systems, solar compatibility, and tough construction. Search for RVs with high ground clearance, freshwater tanks, and lithium battery systems.

Key Decision Criteria:

When you limit down your alternatives, consider the following:

Budget

Initial Costs: The purchase price ranges from around $20,000 for a simple trailer to more than $500,000 for a luxury motorcoach.

Ongoing costs include gasoline, insurance, maintenance, campsite fees, and storage (when not in use).

Size and Weight

Check the driver's license requirements in your state, as well as the towing capability of your car. Larger RVs may be banned on particular routes or campgrounds.

Sleeping and living capacity

Determine the number of passengers and their comfort demands. Bunk beds, convertible dinettes, and slide-outs improve sleeping options.

Driveability vs towability

First-time RVers often favor motorhomes because of their all-in-one design. Experienced travelers may choose towables because of the ability to separate the tow vehicle.

Climate Compatibility

If you want to travel during the colder months, look into four-season packages. Insulated tanks, double-pane windows, and heated underbellies are a few examples.

New versus Used

New RVs.

Advantages include manufacturer warranties, cutting-edge technology, and clean, unused interiors.

Disadvantages: Rapid depreciation during the first two years.

Used RVs

Advantages: Lower cost, often renovated by former owners.

Disadvantages: May need quick repair or system upgrade. Always obtain a professional examination.

The Smart Selection Process

Define your travel mission. Are you looking for seasonal events, state parks, or a yearly cross-country loop? Your route helps to establish your vehicle requirements.

Research and Compare: To learn about layouts and features, visit RV exhibitions, rental websites, and take virtual tours.

Renting various RV models via peer-to-peer services such as Outdoorsy or Cruise America may provide hands-on experience before making a purchase decision.

Plan for Storage and Maintenance: Determine where your RV will be kept during the offseason and who will handle servicing requirements.

Think Ahead: Select a model that will accommodate not just this year's vacation, but the following five.

Pro Tip:

Some tourists regret getting too big or too tiny. A 26-30 foot RV is often considered a "sweet spot" for combining comfort, accessibility, and park compatibility over the majority of the United States.

Choosing the appropriate RV is more than just a personal taste; it's about matching your equipment to the landscapes you want to explore, the speed you want, and the memories you want to make. The better the fit, the easier the voyage.

Packing Smart for the Road

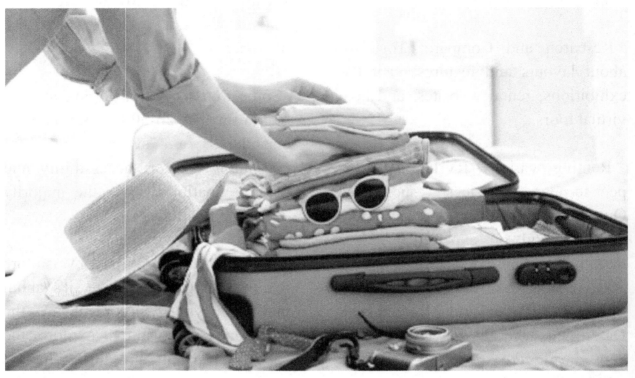

Effective packing is the foundation of a successful RV trip. Every square inch counts. Unlike plane travel, where baggage is stored and forgotten until arrival, RVing requires a careful balance of comfort and weight, accessibility and storage, need and convenience. Packing wisely doesn't imply packing light; it requires packing correctly.

Essentials First: The Non-Negotiables

Before you load cabinets with extras, consider the operational and safety requirements. These are the equipment and materials that keep your RV operating, your campground operational, and your staff safe:

RV toolkit includes an adjustable wrench, pliers, screwdrivers, tire pressure gauge, duct tape, bungee cords, zip ties, multimeter, and a small power drill.

Sewage and water equipment includes a quality sewage hose with a transparent elbow, hose support, disposable gloves, a fresh water hose (ideally safe for drinking), a water pressure regulator, a water filter, and tank treatment pods.

Electrical requirements include a heavy-duty extension cable, surge protector, 30/50 amp adaptor (depending on setup), additional fuses, and an energy monitoring system.

For manual stabilizer jacks, use wheel chocks, leveling blocks, bubble levels, or smartphone leveling applications, as well as a crank or cordless drill.

Emergency Kit: First-aid kit, fire extinguisher, flares or emergency triangles, flashlight with additional batteries, thermal blankets, and a weather radio.

Kitchen configuration: A Rolling Galley of Efficiency.

Your kitchen should be designed to be small, functional, and clutter-free, similar to a minimalist chef's station.

Cookware includes stackable nonstick pots and pans with retractable handles, a collapsible colander, nested mixing bowls, and a slow cooker or Instant Pot (ideal for one-pot RV cooking).

Utensils and Tools: Magnetic knife strip, multifunctional can/bottle opener, drip-edged cutting board, measuring spoons/cups, and silicone spatulas.

Airtight containers, zip-lock bags, mason jars, and under-cabinet baskets let you make the most of your pantry space.

Salt, pepper, oil, sugar, wheat, rice, pasta, canned products, and flavor packages are all essential ingredients. For perishables, organize them in a "use first" box.

Cleaning supplies include a compact dish rack, biodegradable dish soap, microfiber towels, scrub brushes, and rubbish bags appropriate for your bin size.

Clothing Strategy: Pack for layers, not outfits.
Weather may vary greatly across states, or even within hours. Create a travel outfit that focuses on adaptability rather than volume.

Base layers include moisture-wicking shirts, leggings, and thermal underwear.

Midlayers include fleece, hoodies, and lightweight sweaters.

Outerwear: windbreaker, rain jacket, and packable insulated jacket.

Footwear options include hiking boots, waterproof slip-ons, and camp shoes.

Multipurpose accessories include buffs, caps, gloves, and quick-dry towels.

washing Preparation: A collapsible washing basket, travel-size detergent, quarters or laundry cards, and spot removal pens.

Bedding and Bath: Home Comforts on the Go

Space-saving comfort is essential. Consider modular, washable, and quick-drying.

Bedding includes fitted RV-sized sheets, all-season duvets or sleeping bags, throw blankets, and a memory foam mattress topper for improved sleep quality.

Bathroom supplies include quick-dry towels, washcloths, over-the-door hanging organizers, shower shoes, and biodegradable toiletries.

Toilet supplies include RV-safe toilet paper, tank deodorizer tabs, and a brush with a sealed holder.

Living Smart: Entertainment, Connectivity, and Daily Life.

Life on the road is more than just campfires and canyon vistas; everyday comforts are important.

Wi-Fi booster, hotspot device, signal extender, and USB-enabled charging station.

Entertainment options include foldable table games, an e-reader, a Bluetooth speaker, or a streaming gadget.

Workspace (if required): Laptop tray, folding desk, and privacy curtain for virtual meetings or remote working.

Outdoor Gear: Extend Your Living Space
Your RV is just the hub; to really appreciate it, consider outside the walls.

Camp Setup: Folding chairs, an outside mat, mosquito repellent lights, a pop-up canopy or awning, and posts or sandbags.

Grilling and Dining: Portable barbecue, grill equipment, propane cylinders, picnic table, and foldable cooler.

Binoculars, fishing rod, bikes and helmets, trekking poles, and an inflatable kayak or paddleboard if space permits.

Storage Solutions: Solving the Space Puzzle.

Strategic packing relies on utilizing space with purpose. Invest in the appropriate organizational tools:

Drawer dividers prevent utensils and tiny equipment from jumbling.

Over-the-Door Hooks: Perfect for coats, towels, and luggage.

Clear Bins: Stackable and see-through for optimal pantry and under-bed storage.

Velcro Strips and Bungee Cords: Secure goods during travel and keep clutter under control.

Under-seat compartments are ideal for storing shoes, extra linens, or bulk dry items.

Paperwork and Planning Materials

Digital is useful, but paper does not need a signal. Keep a waterproof folder or fireproof document bag on board.

Driver's license and passports

RV Registration and Insurance

Roadside assistance membership information

Printed maps and route plans.

Reservation Confirmations

Emergency contact list

Packing smartly is a skill that is constantly evolving. Each trip builds on the one before it. Revisit your list on a regular basis and fine-tune your system based on the regions you visit, the seasons you travel in, and how you live while on the road. Think modular, multi-use, and always look a few miles ahead.

Safety Tips & Emergency Prep

Whether traveling through high-altitude passes in the Rockies, risking desert seclusion in the Southwest, or exploring wooded back roads in the Pacific Northwest, safety is a constant companion for all RVers. This chapter is designed to serve as your front-line toolkit—practical, scenario-specific, and adaptable to any sort of rig, climate, or road condition you'll encounter in the US. Read it before you leave, then go over it again before each leg of the trip.

1. Essential Onboard Safety Equipment.

Equipping your RV entails more than just stocking cabinets with electronics. Prioritize the following gear, sorted according to function:

Fire and Electricity:

ABC-rated fire extinguishers: at least one near the kitchen, one near the bedroom, and one accessible via outdoor storage.

Surge protector with EMS (Electrical Management System): Prevents voltage spikes in campsites.

Smoke, carbon monoxide, and propane detectors: Test regularly and replace batteries twice a year.

Mechanical:

Hydraulic jack rated for your truck's GVWR.

Heavy-duty lug wrench and tire repair kit.

Torque wrench calibrated for your wheel specifications.

Navigation and Signaling:

Reflective warning triangles and LED road flares

Battery-powered weather radio (NOAA-certified)

High-lumen flashlight with a backup battery.

Medical:

First-aid kit should include trauma shears, antiseptics, antihistamines, and a tick removal tool.

Back up medications in properly labeled containers.

Medical identification cards for all tourists, including blood type and allergies.

2. Know before you tow (or drive).

Safety starts with situational awareness. Each journey requires reconnaissance:

Check Route Restrictions.

RV-specific GPS programs or atlases may help you avoid low-clearance bridges, propane-restricted tunnels, and tight bends.

Check state DOT websites for construction delays and road closures.

Weather Awareness:

Understand the regional threats: tornadoes in the Midwest, black ice in the Northeast, and wildfires in the West.

Set up location alerts using applications such as MyRadar or Windy to get real-time information.

Weight and load:

Visit a CAT scale to weigh your RV (axle by axle). Brakes and suspension are put under stress when the Gross Combined Weight Rating (GCWR) is exceeded.

Redistribute the weight such that the center of gravity remains low and central.

3. Emergency Procedures Based on Environment

Mountain passes:

Downshift before descending and never use the brakes.

If your brakes overheat, pull over immediately—rolling smoke signals an impending failure.

Desert Roads:

Carry at least one gallon of water per person each day, with a three-day supply.

Never depend only on cell signals; satellite messengers such as Garmin inReach provide SOS capabilities off-grid.

Urban Zones:

Avoid traveling through cities at rush hour, particularly with trailers or fifth wheels.

Never leave your RV alone in unmonitored lots overnight; instead, park near well-lit, 24-hour enterprises as needed.

Flood and Storm Zones:

Never drive over standing water—even six inches will halt most automobiles.

During strong storms, avoid parking beneath trees or near powerlines.

4. Roadside Breakdown Protocol

Step by Step Response Plan:

Pull over safely. Use the shoulder or emergency bay. Avoid slopes and blind turns.

Place reflectors at 10-, 100-, and 200-foot intervals behind the truck.

Check for fire hazards: If you smell gasoline or see smoke, leave.

Call for help: Know your position (mile marker or GPS coordinates).

Describe the vehicle's kind, symptoms, and number of passengers.

Keep your hazard lights on. Use luminous vests while leaving the car at night.

Maintain a roadside assistance membership specifically for RVs (such as Coach-Net or Good Sam), rather than simply normal vehicle coverage.

5. Emergency Preparedness Checklist (Monthly Review)

■ Check tire pressure and tread, including the spare.

■ Test smoke, CO, and propane alarms.

■ Fill all fluid levels (engine, transmission, and braking)

■ Replenish water and non-perishable food stock (3-day minimum)

■ Check backup power sources (generator, solar, or battery bank) to ensure proper operation.

■ Check for outdated drugs or supplies.

Store a printed binder with the following:

Copies of car insurance and registration

Roadside service contact information

Medical summary for all travelers.

Paper maps include principal and alternative routes.

6. RV-Specific Emergency Plans

Evacuation readiness:

Keep the driver's seat clear at all times to ensure a rapid departure.

Keep shoes, keys, and wallets near exits.

Learn how to release slide-outs and stabilize jacks rapidly.

Generator and Propane Safety:

Always turn off propane while refilling or traveling through tunnels.

Never run a generator in a confined space or when the wind blows exhaust near the rig.

Wildlife Encounters:

Use bear-proof containers as necessary.

Food should never be stored overnight in soft-sided pop-ups or beneath awnings in bear country.

7. Mental preparation: practice scenarios.

Run through the drills:

Simulate a tire blowout: how do you react without overcorrecting?

Assign family duties for fire evacuation: who collects the pets and who phones for help?

Determine how quickly you can transition from shore power to generator during an outage.

Confidence is gained via practice. When the unexpected occurs, you will rely on your training rather than fear.

Conclusion:

The journey is enormous, as are the variables. Preparation is often the distinguishing factor between a diversion and a tragedy. With this chapter as your operational baseline, you're not simply wishing for the best; you're preparing for it. The RV lifestyle rewards those who prepare like a pilot and drive like an experienced scout. Keep your gear sharp, your mind keen, and your route smooth.

RV Etiquette & Campground Rules

From coastal campgrounds to mountain pullouts: the unspoken codes and official expectations that keep the RV community rolling smoothly.

Whether you're a seasoned full-timer or embarking on your first cross-country trip, learning RV etiquette and park laws is critical for preserving peace on the road and at campgrounds. Beyond the official signs and written restrictions, there is a code of civility developed over decades of shared spaces, tiny back-ins, and fireside conversations. Respect these ideals, and doors—and campsite gates—will open with a grin.

1. Respect the Quiet Hours: Silence fosters serenity.
Nearly every campsite has designated quiet hours, which are typically

between 10:00 p.m. and 6:00 or 7:00 a.m. These hours are not recommendations; they are posted for a purpose. Keep the volume moderate, turn off noisy generators, and reserve the karaoke machine for another occasion. Sound travels further in open spaces than it does in fenced-in communities, and the desert solitude or woodland calm intensifies even little disturbances.

Best Practice: If you arrive late, lower the lights, minimize slamming doors, and postpone complete setup until the morning. Other travelers need rest just as much as you do.

2. Generator Use: Power with Prudence

Generators are often used for power in off-grid camping, but their usage should be considered carefully. Many campsites have set generator operating hours, which are generally from mid-morning until early evening. Even in scattered regions, excessive generating noise might disrupt the calm environment for others.

Tip: Invest in a quiet inverter generator and utilize solar panels wherever feasible. These initiatives

generate goodwill and help your neighbors sleep better.

3. Site Boundaries: Respect the Invisible Lines.

Campgrounds are demarcated spaces. Parking your tow vehicle, extending your awning, or strolling your dogs across someone else's campsite breaches an unwritten rule as ancient as RVing: remain in your lane. Sites are personal areas, not thoroughfares or shortcuts.

Rule of thumb: If you wouldn't stroll over someone's front yard in a neighborhood, don't do so at a campsite.

4. Leave No Trace: Clean Campsites Increase Community Trust.

Cleaning isn't simply polite; it's necessary. Always dispose of garbage correctly, never dump gray or black water anywhere other than approved stations, and keep cans, plastics, and food waste out of fire pits. Wild creatures are attracted to remains, and improper disposal jeopardizes campsite access for everyone.

Checklist before departure:

Trash packaged and discarded.

Fire pit is cool and clean.

Sewer pipes are properly stored

Site restored to its pre-arrival condition—or better.

5. Hookups and Hoses: Do It Properly and Safely

Water and electrical connections need accuracy. To prevent trip risks, ensure that hoses and cables are in excellent shape, firmly linked, and neatly routed. Avoid letting sewage hoses leak or touching drinking water hoses.

Color Code Tip: For potable water, use a white hose and a separate black or gray line for cleansing tanks. Store them individually.

6. Campfire: Flames with Boundaries

Fire regulations vary according to area and season. Before lighting up, check for any local burn restrictions or laws. Use existing fire rings and keep flames small in size. Never leave a fire unattended, and always use water to completely extinguish it—not soil or a fast stomp.

Fire Wisdom: A responsible fire promotes warmth and community. Being reckless brings risk and sanctions.

7. Pet Behavior: Tail-Wagging with Courtesy

Dogs are wonderful RV companions, but they must always be leashed, managed, and cleaned up after. Excessive barking is a typical cause of campsite complaints. If your pet has a tendency to vocalize, try indoor enrichment or noise-blocking measures.

Unwritten rule: Put pet waste bags in your pocket before you need them, not after. Always dispose of them correctly.

8. Speed Limits: Slow Wheels and Safe Spaces

Campground speed restrictions often range from 5 to 10 mph. Children, cats, bicycles, and other RVers move unexpectedly, therefore they're set low. Dust clouds on gravel roads and tight corners in forested areas need vigilance.

If your wheels kick up dust or your engine drowns out talk, you're going too fast.

9. Socialization: Friendly, Not Forceful.

Many RVers enjoy the company of park living, but not everyone seeks a fireside talk. Greet neighbors, provide assistance when necessary, and respect social boundaries. Invitations to socialize should be pleasant and not persistent.

Etiquette Tip: Only knock on a door if required. Otherwise, wait for a communal spot, such as a picnic area or trailhead, to start a discussion.

10. Departure Strategy: Early Birds with Tact.

Leaving a place early? Keep noise to a minimum. Avoid screaming, slamming compartments, or operating diesel engines for lengthy periods of time before 7:00 a.m. Many people plan their trips before daybreak, but careful preparation the night before might help to minimize the early chaos.

Departure Tip: Finish external setup (tire checks, connections, awning retraction) without disturbing the surrounding environment.

11. Dump Station Decorum: Flow Efficiency

When utilizing a disposal station, be efficient and considerate. Long lines and scorching days might test your patience. Prepare gloves and materials before your turn. Do not use the place for tank rinsing or casual talk.

The Golden Rule states that you should clean up after oneself. Leave the station prepared for the next RVer.

12. Long-term and seasonal sites: blend in, do not stand out.

If you're there for a lengthy amount of time, keep your space clean. Keep the site clean, reduce visual effect (e.g., storage mounds, clotheslines, unnecessary décor), and keep the rig in excellent shape. Permanent-looking structures can violate park restrictions and community expectations.

Visual Rule: Your website should portray movement rather than permanency.

Conclusion: the unspoken grid that connects us.

RV life relies on mutual respect. The lifestyle allows you freedom, but it also comes with responsibilities. Etiquette is more than simply being nice; it is about ensuring that everyone has the opportunity to enjoy the benefits of road life. Learn the rules, respect the area, and go forward with decency. The path is long, the community is vast, and decent manners never go out of style.

Chapter 2: Planning the Perfect RV Trip

Route Planning Basics

Precision route planning lays the groundwork for a safe, picturesque, and enjoyable RV vacation. While spontaneity has its appeal, the reality of driving a home-on-wheels across vast and diverse American landscapes needs foresight. The following essentials can help you simplify travel, increase fuel economy, and decrease stress while enjoying every mile of the experience.

1. Know Your RV Specifications Before You Roll

Before mapping a path, take note of your RV's dimensions and weight. Clearance height, total length (including tow vehicle or pulled trailer), breadth, turning radius, and gross vehicle weight rating (GVWR) are all important measurements. Many rural roads, tunnels, and bridges, particularly those in older towns and hilly areas, are restricted. Crossing a 10-foot clearance with a 12-foot rig is not an error that can be corrected.

Checklist:

Height (including rooftop attachments)

Length (with trailer or tow)

Width (with the mirrors extended)

Weight (full load)

Apps like RV LIFE and CoPilot RV incorporate these data into safe, RV-specific routing.

2. Select the Right Mapping Tools.

Not all GPS devices are made equal for RV travel. Commercial trucking routes and RV-specific navigators provide customized information such as steep gradients, propane limits, and servicing stations. Paper atlases, such as the Rand McNally Motor Carriers' Road Atlas or this handbook, are essential backups in places with poor signal.

Recommended tools:

GPS with RV mode (such as Garmin RV Series)

Offline-capable map applications

printed atlas with elevation and service markings.

Park directory guidelines (e.g., Good Sam and KOA)

3. Segment the journey. Strategically, long-haul RVing is not a race. Divide the journey into reasonable segments—ideally, no more than 300 miles or five hours each day. Plan for slower speeds, fuel stops, food breaks, and unexpected diversions. Avoid late-day arrivals at campsites, when visibility is reduced and setup becomes more challenging.

Optimal Planning Formula:

330 Rule: Drive no more than 330 miles per day or arrive by 3:30 PM, whichever occurs sooner.

Plan relaxation days every 3-5 travel days.

Combine driving days with lengthy stays in beautiful or activity-rich locations.

4. Identify Overnight Options in Advance.

Overnight alternatives range greatly in availability, facilities, and expense, from full-service RV parks to basic boondocking sites. Reservations at popular campsites, particularly those near national parks, sometimes fill months in advance. Apps like Campendium, Harvest Hosts, and Recreation.gov enable you to sort by rig size, connection type, and pricing. Always call ahead of time for last-minute stays.

Common Overnight Types:

Public campsites (state and national parks)

Private RV Parks and Resorts

Boondocking on BLM lands

Overnight parking is permitted at Walmart, Cracker Barrel, and various casinos.

5. Route around Weather, Traffic, and Terrain

Weather is more than simply an annoyance; it can be dangerous. Prepare for hurricane season in the Southeast, snow in the Rockies, and wildfire-prone places in the West. Before leaving for the day, use radar and weather forecasting tools. Avoid steep gradients in cold weather and reroute away from construction-heavy metro lines during peak hours.

Key Resources:

NOAA and AccuWeather provide regional predictions.

Windy.com provides graphic wind maps (essential for high-profile RVs).

511 traffic information websites for each state.

Mountain Directory East and West (Print and Digital)

6. Create a flexible itinerary.

Flexibility is as vital as structure. Plan A should always be accompanied by a backup plan. Make allowances in the timetable for delays, diversions, or unexpected local discoveries. Keep printed notes or offline digital copies of route, contact, and camping information. Avoid "overbooking" the journey with daily deadlines that deplete the pleasure of discovery.

Tips for Adaptive Planning:

Pad each day with a time buffer.

Save offline copies of instructions and confirmation emails.

Maintain a printed travel journal that includes mileage, fuel stops, and contacts.

Know alternative paths between essential locations.

7. Fuel Stops and Service Planning.
Gas station access for big RVs is not ubiquitous. Look for truck stops and RV-friendly stations on major interstates and highways. Fuel stops in distant places should be planned ahead of time. Diesel rig operators should double-check DEF availability. If you're going long distances, look for approved service locations for your RV brand.

Considerations:

Plan to refuel every 200-300 miles.

Use applications like GasBuddy and iExit to find truck-accessible stations.

Note RV service dealers along the route in case of problems.

8. Understand State Laws and Limits
States have different bridge laws, overnight parking requirements, trailer speed limits, and RV-specific limitations (e.g., propane restrictions in tunnels). This may have an impact on routing, particularly in the Northeast and major areas such as New York City and Chicago.

Essential Checks:

State-specific RV length and towing regulations

Propane limits (such as the Baltimore Harbor Tunnel)

Toll road and EZPass compatibility.

Open carry or weapon transportation rules

9. Balancing Interstate Efficiency and Scenic Byways
Interstates provide speed and convenience, but America's most memorable trips are generally along two-lane roads and designated scenic routes. Include America's Byways®, Historic Route 66, the Blue Ridge Parkway, or the Pacific Coast Highway on your journey for breathtaking scenery.

Scenic Highlights to Consider:

Mississippi River (Great River Road)

Natchez Trace Parkway (from Mississippi to Tennessee)

Highway 12: Utah's Scenic Byway.

US Route 101 (Pacific Coast).

Always certain that the picturesque road you choose is passable and safe for RVs of your size.

10. Final Checklist Before Departure. A great plan includes more than just outlining the route. Every travel day, go through a complete pre-trip checklist.

Departure Readiness Checklist:

Confirm the route, fuel, and camping bookings.

Inspect the tires, lights, fluids, and hitch connections.

Secure inside goods and shut slide-outs.

Check the weather and traffic reports.

Notify travel companions or emergency contact about the day's itinerary.

A skillfully planned route is more than just a path from point A to point B; it is the foundation for the whole trip. RVers can turn lengthy highways into unforgettable journeys around America with careful preparation, flexible execution, and the correct gear.

Boondocking vs. Campgrounds

Understanding the difference between boondocking and typical campsites is critical for RV travelers planning their trip throughout the United States. It allows them to adapt their experience to their tastes, budget, and adventurous style. Both methods have distinct benefits and problems, impacting route planning, daily logistics, and overall trip happiness.

What is boondocking?

Boondocking, also known as dry camping, is camping without connections, which means no direct access to power, water, or sewage services. This kind of camping occurs mostly on public lands controlled by the Bureau of Land Management (BLM), National Forests, or other scattered camping locations. It may also occur on private property with authorization.

Key Characteristics:

Self-sufficiency: When boondocking, you must rely on your RV's internal resources, which include freshwater tanks, batteries, solar panels, and trash storage. Preparation and resource management are key.

Cost savings: Because boondocking places are either free or offer a little fee, this alternative significantly decreases overnight expenses.

Privacy & solitude: Dispersed camping areas are less crowded, providing a more peaceful experience surrounded by nature.

Flexibility: Because there are no reservation restrictions, boondockers may quickly change places and adjust their itinerary on the fly.

Considerations:

Limited amenities: The lack of connections means no power, running water, or toilet facilities. Campers must provide for potable water, electricity, and waste disposal.

Accessibility: Some scattered locations may need off-road capabilities or the ability to navigate unimproved roads.

Environmental responsibility: Following Leave No Trace guidelines is critical for protecting fragile habitats and ensuring access for future campers.

Legal restrictions: Not all public lands allow overnight visits; check local legislation, maximum stay limitations, and designated zones.

What are campgrounds?

Campgrounds provide designated sites with varied degrees of amenities, ranging from basic tent sites to full-service RV parks with 30/50 amp electricity connections, water, sewage, Wi-Fi, and recreational facilities.

Key Characteristics:

Amenities and convenience: Campgrounds often provide consistent access to utilities, making living on the road more pleasant and decreasing the need for resource management.

Security and services: Many campsites provide personnel, security patrols, dump stations, laundry facilities, and sometimes community events.

Reservation systems: Campgrounds often demand reservations, particularly during high seasons, which allows for ahead planning but limits spontaneity.

Campgrounds promote community via shared areas and group activities, making them ideal for tourists seeking connection.

Considerations:

Costs: Full-service campgrounds vary greatly in price, with major tourist destinations fetching higher prices.

Crowds: During holidays and weekends, campsites may fill up rapidly, resulting in loud or crowded circumstances.

Location: Campgrounds are often concentrated near famous attractions or major highways, limiting access to more remote or off-the-beaten-path locations.

Choosing between boondocking and camping.

The selection is based on lifestyle preferences, travel objectives, and practical limits. Here are various variables to consider while choosing overnight options:

Factor	Boondocking	Campgrounds
Cost	Low or free	Varies; from budget to premium
Privacy	High; isolated sites	Variable; more crowded
Amenities	Minimal to none	Full-service options available
Accessibility	May require off-road driving	Generally easy access
Planning	Flexible, spontaneous	Often requires advance booking
Environmental Impact	Requires careful stewardship	Facilities minimize impact
Power and Water	Self-supplied	Hookups available

Expert Advice for Balancing Both

Mix and match: To combine isolation with comfort, many RVers switch between boondocking and campsites, particularly on extended travels.

Scout ahead: To find appropriate stops along your trip, use boondocking-specific apps and maps, as well as campground databases.

Upgrade your rig: Installing solar panels, bigger water tanks, and efficient waste systems improves boondocking feasibility.

Respect the land: To ensure camping access, carefully adhere to fire laws, trash disposal guidelines, and site constraints.

Plan for recharge: Even boondockers may need periodic access to campsites to recharge batteries, replenish water tanks, and dump tanks.

Understanding the differences between boondocking and campsites enables RVers to plan road trips that balance adventure, convenience, and sustainability. Whether you like the raw freedom of the open wilderness or the luxury of well-appointed campsites, the road offers limitless alternatives.

Budgeting for Fuel, Campsites & More

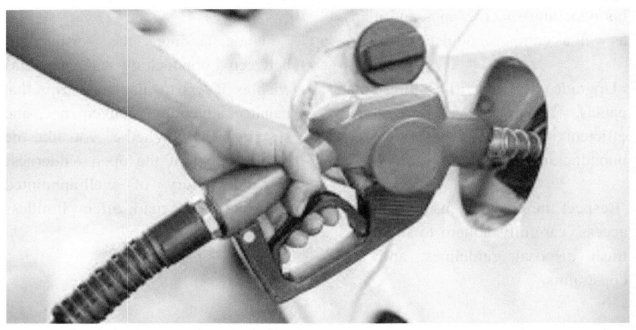

Effective budgeting is the foundation of every successful RV excursion, ensuring that the road is as joyful as the destination. Understanding and forecasting the prices of gasoline, campgrounds, and other necessities is critical for the 2025 road tripper to keep both financial management and peace of mind while on the road.

Fuel Costs: Planning for the Largest Expense

Fuel is always one of the most expensive items on any lengthy RV journey. RVs' sheer size and weight often result in poorer miles per gallon than passenger cars, making fuel budgeting an important factor.

Understand Your Vehicle's Efficiency: Start by calculating your RV's typical fuel use. This may vary greatly—from around 6 miles per gallon for big Class A motorhomes to 10-15 miles per gallon for smaller Class C or travel trailers towed by fuel-efficient tow cars. Accurate fuel economy statistics may be obtained from manufacturer specs or real-world user reports.

Map Out Mileage: Once the proposed route has been sketched, calculate total miles to determine fuel requirements. Distances may be measured using online mapping tools and RV-specific navigation applications, which also take into account diversions and picturesque byways.

Account for Fuel Price Variability: Fuel costs vary regionally and seasonally. California and the Northeast often experience higher per-gallon rates than the Midwest or Southern areas. To account for these swings, include a buffer in your gasoline budget—adding 10-15% over the current average price might help avoid shocks.

Use Fuel Rewards and Apps: Many truck stops and gas stations have fuel rewards programs that may lower per-gallon prices. Furthermore, RV-specific applications may help you find the lowest gasoline stations along your trip, allowing for more strategic filling stops.

Campsite Expenses: Deciding Between Comfort and Cost

Campsite costs vary greatly based on location, facilities, and the time of year. Budgeting effectively for overnight stays is critical for controlling total travel expenditures.

National and state parks often provide some of the most gorgeous and serene camping alternatives, with fees ranging from $20 to $50 per night for full hookups. Reservations are advised far in advance, particularly during high seasons, to obtain sites at these popular destinations.

Private campgrounds may include a variety of amenities, including Wi-Fi, laundry, swimming pools, and more. Rates might vary from $30 to more than $70 per night, but many offer amenities that improve the whole experience.

Boondocking and Dispersed Camping: For RVers wishing to save expenditures, boondocking (camping without hookups) in approved areas or public lands maintained by the Bureau of Land Management (BLM) is a feasible option. These places are often free or very low-cost, although they have few facilities and demand self-sufficiency.

Membership Discounts: Organizations like Good Sam Club,

Passport America, and Escapees RV Club provide reduced prices at connected parks. Investing in a membership might result in significant savings over the course of a lengthy journey.

Additional Budget Considerations:

Aside from fuel and campsites, several other expenses should be included in the budget to avoid surprises.

Propane is necessary for heating, cooking, and refrigeration in many RVs. Costs vary depending on area and consumption, but plan to replenish propane tanks numerous times during a cross-country journey.

Maintenance and Repairs: Regular maintenance, such as oil changes, tire inspections, and unforeseen repairs, need the putting aside of finances. A suggested safety net is 5-10% of the overall trip budget allocated to maintenance.

Groceries and Dining: Cooking aboard saves money, but experiencing local cuisine periodically adds to the voyage experience. Set aside a flexible food budget that balances both.

Admission Fees and Activities: National parks, museums, and attractions frequently charge admission fees. Prioritize must-see destinations and factor in the associated costs.

connecting and Entertainment: While many RV parks have Wi-Fi, connecting may need a mobile hotspot or data plan upgrade, which should be budgeted for if working remotely or streaming entertainment.

By anticipating these fundamental expenditures and allowing for strategic flexibility, RV travelers can concentrate on what really matters—exploring the open road, finding hidden treasures, and enjoying the freedom of America's various landscapes. Sound financial preparedness transforms every mile traveled into a confident and enjoyable experience.

Seasonal Travel Tips

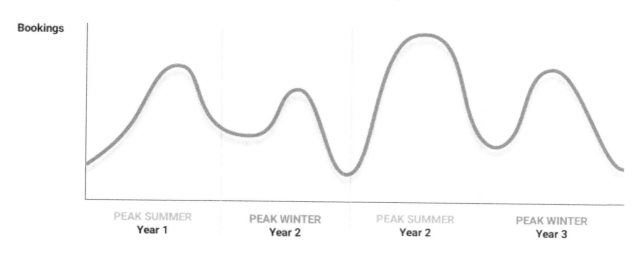

Navigating the United States in an RV requires careful consideration of seasonal fluctuations, since weather, road conditions, and regional attractions change dramatically throughout the year. To maximize comfort, safety, and pleasure, you must first understand how each season influences your vacation and the sites you will visit.

Spring: Awakening Adventures and Blooming Landscapes.

Spring brings mild temperatures and beautiful landscapes, making it a perfect time for RV travel. Southern areas such as Florida, Texas, and Arizona have favorable weather, which encourages early departures from colder northern regions still melting from winter's hold.

Road Conditions: Melting snow and intermittent rain in northern states may result in muddy or slippery sections on minor routes. Primary roadways are often clean, although early spring storms might impede traffic.

Crowds and Reservations: National and state parks begin to fill, especially around Easter and spring break.

Advance bookings for camping are strongly advised.

Wildlife and Nature: This season brings beautiful wildflower blooming and busy wildlife observations. Beautiful natural hues may be seen along the Blue Ridge Parkway and in California's wine area.

Packing Essentials: Bring rain gear, layered clothes for changing temperatures, and insect repellant as pests emerge with warmer weather.

Summer: Peak Exploration and High Traffic.
Summer is peak RV travel season, with long daylight hours and numerous festivals and events attracting crowds across the country.

Traffic and Camping: Popular roads, such as the Pacific Coast Highway, the Great Smoky Mountains, and Yellowstone, see significant traffic and crowded campsites. Early morning departures and weekday travel assist to reduce congestion.

Heat considerations: Temperatures in the southern and desert areas may be quite high. Make sure your RV's cooling system works properly, and schedule stops with access to shade and water. Monsoon storms are common in the Southwest during early summer; keep a watchful eye on the weather.

Summer school vacations lead to an increase in family and group travel. Larger group campsites provide social possibilities, although quieter areas may need more effort to locate.

Fuel & Supplies: Due to longer travel distances and limited rural amenities, it is necessary to arrange fuel stops and provisions ahead of time.

Autumn Colors and Cooler Comforts
Autumn is a captivating travel season, marked by beautiful foliage, cool air, and often less tourists.

Scenic Routes: Well-known roads such as New England's Route 100, the Great River Road along the Mississippi, and the Appalachian Trail circuits highlight peak autumn colors.

Temperatures start to plummet, particularly in the north and mountains. Nighttime freezes may occur, necessitating RV winterization inspections.

Harvest and Festival Season: Autumn harvest festivals, wine tastings, and cultural activities augment the trip experience. Planning around them might offer a distinct local character to your schedule.

Reduced Services: After Labor Day, certain seasonal campsites and attractions shut; check availability in advance.

Winter: Off-season Challenges and Serene Landscapes.

Winter travel requires more preparation, but it provides unsurpassed seclusion and the opportunity to visit warmer areas.

Southern States Advantage: Regions such as Florida, southern California, and the Southwest have become popular winter escapes, with several RV parks catering to travelers.

Cold Weather Risks: In northern latitudes and mountain passes, snow, ice, and road closures are prevalent. Check for winter driving warnings and avoid unplowed backroads.

RV Heating and Insulation: Reliable heating systems and insulated tanks are essential. Carry additional supplies such as warm clothes,

emergency blankets, and enough food and drink.

Lower Costs and Availability: Winter often brings lower rates and plenty of camping space, while services may be restricted. Book early for popular warm-weather getaways.

General Seasonal Navigation Advice:
Monitor weather forecasts: Real-time information and notifications are critical year-round for making safe travel choices.

Flexible Itinerary Planning: Seasonal closures and circumstances need adaptive routes and contingency preparations.

Vehicle Maintenance: Seasonal transitions are ideal seasons for complete RV inspections, including tire, brake, heating/cooling system, and fluid levels.

Local rules: Weight limitations on roadways, fire prohibitions, and other rules vary by state and season. Consult official sources routinely.

RV explorers may maximize the potential of America's unique landscapes by incorporating seasonal insights into their planning and

everyday travel choices, making each
journey enjoyable and stress-free.

Accessibility & Pet-Friendly Travel

Traveling around the United States by RV provides unequaled independence, but maintaining comfort for all travelers—particularly those with mobility requirements or animal companions—requires careful preparation. The 2025 version of the USA RVers Road Atlas offers crucial assistance for navigating the country's numerous accessibility and pet-friendly alternatives, ensuring that every trip is joyful, inclusive, and hassle-free.

Accessibility for All: Navigating Easily

The wide American environment offers a range of terrains and services, making accessibility an important consideration in route planning and destination selection. Many national parks, state parks, and campsites have greatly enhanced accessible infrastructure to meet Americans with Disabilities Act (ADA) criteria. Travelers should anticipate paved or hard surface walkways, accessible toilets, and parking areas specifically designed for mobility device users.

Campgrounds and RV Parks: Look for ADA-compliant sites with level ground, larger parking spaces, and accessible connections. Many large campsite chains and government-operated parks provide accessibility information online, frequently including maps of accessible pathways and common spaces.

Road Conditions and Scenic Routes: Although scenic routes provide beautiful vistas, some roads remain tough owing to restricted lanes, steep hills, or gravel surfaces. The atlas recommends other routes that provide a mix between accessibility and scenic value, including paved, well-maintained highways ideal for all RV sizes and mobility needs.

Visitor centers, rest rooms, and attractions usually include ramps, elevators, and accessible observation platforms. Planning stops at areas with these features improves the experience of passengers with physical restrictions.

Assistive Services: Many parks and communities provide mobility device rentals, accessible transportation, and guided tours for guests with disabilities. The atlas highlights these services, recommending prior bookings if feasible.

Traveling with Pets: Welcome Companions on the Road.

Bringing dogs along enhances the RV experience, but understanding pet rules and locating appropriate facilities is critical to ensuring their safety and pleasure.

Pet-Friendly campsites: An increasing number of campsites in the United States specifically cater to pet owners, with dedicated off-leash areas, pet waste facilities, and surrounding trails. The atlas offers detailed lists of pet-friendly campgrounds, including leash requirements, breed limitations (if any), and facility characteristics such as dog wash facilities or pet-friendly food choices nearby.

Pets are typically allowed in state and national parks, but there are laws in place to safeguard animals and ecosystems. Typically, dogs must be leashed and limited to built places such as campsites and paved pathways. The atlas breaks out these restrictions state by state to assist tourists avoid unintended breaches.

Pet Travel Tips: To keep pets comfortable when traveling, use routes with frequent rest stations and shady locations. The atlas emphasizes routes with well-equipped rest areas that include pet hydration stations, exercise spaces, and secure fencing.

Veterinary Services and Emergencies: Unexpected health problems might emerge on the road. The atlas depicts major veterinarian clinics, emergency animal hospitals, and 24-hour pet pharmacies along popular RV routes, allowing quick access to treatment.

Integrating accessibility and pet friendliness

Achieving a balance between accessibility and pet friendliness is critical to a smooth RV vacation. Many places now include these factors, including accessible dog parks, pet relieving areas near accessible facilities, and broad paths ideal for mobility aids and leash walks.

For individuals traveling with both mobility requirements and pets, the atlas suggests:

Prioritizing campsites that provide both ADA-compliant sites and pet amenities.

Confirming exact site layouts and adjacent facilities by direct contact before arrival.

Using technology, such as applications and websites dedicated to accessible, pet-friendly travel, in conjunction with the atlas to provide real-time updates.

RVers may enjoy the finest of America's roads with convenience, dignity, and companionship if they master accessibility and pet-friendly alternatives via careful preparation. The USA RVers Road Atlas 2025 is a reliable companion, allowing travelers to comfortably explore every mile with their loved ones—human and animal alike.

Chapter 3: Scenic Byways & Iconic Routes

Pacific Coast Highway (CA to WA)

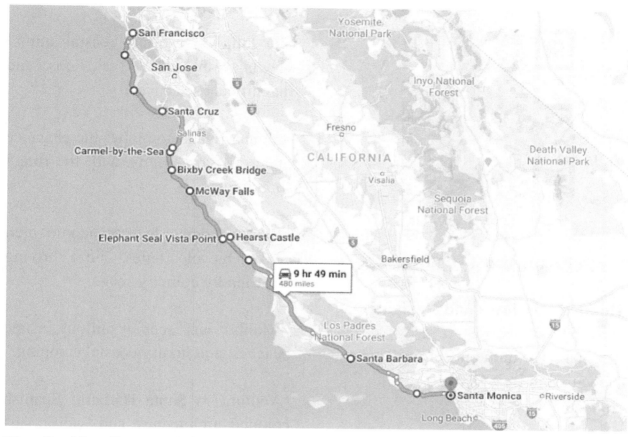

The Pacific Coast Highway (PCH) stretches from the sun-drenched coasts of Southern California to the mist-veiled woods of Washington's Olympic Peninsula, providing RV travelers with a cinematic ribbon of road unlike any other. This fabled road, which consists mostly of California State road 1, U.S. Highway 101, and Washington's picturesque byways, unfolds a coastal symphony of cliffside panoramas, attractive seaside communities, and ecological marvels. The trek covers around 1,650 miles and crosses three states, each with its own pace, landscape, and riches.

This book separates the PCH into logical sections, emphasizing must-see stops, great RV campgrounds, practical navigation recommendations, and detour-worthy attractions.

SCAN THE QR CODE

Pacific Coast Highway

Route Breakdown and Navigation

Segment 1: Southern California (San Diego to San Luis Obispo).

Approximately 300 miles.
Primary route: Interstate 5 to CA-1 (Pacific Coast Highway).

Key Stops:

La Jolla Cove offers coastal animal viewing, including sea lions and magnificent sea caves.

Laguna Beach combines the elegance of an art community with the rough shoreline.

Santa Monica has an iconic pier, coastal bicycle routes, and a thriving RV-friendly culinary scene.

Malibu has scenic pullouts, state beaches, and luxury coastal camping.

Ventura to Santa Barbara: Spanish colonial architecture and Pacific surf moods.

Pismo Beach has coastal dunes, Monarch butterfly forests (seasonal), and beachfront RV resorts.

RV Notes:

Traffic congestion in Los Angeles may be intense. Plan early morning departures.

Height and weight limits apply to certain CA-1 portions; see Caltrans notifications.

During busy seasons, reserve RV sites in the Santa Barbara region months in advance.

Segment 2: Central to Northern California (From San Luis Obispo to Crescent City)

Northern CA Zone

Other Zone

SCAN THE QR CODE

San Luis Obispo to Crescent City)

Distance: Approximately 500 miles.
Primary route: CA-1 to US-101.

Key Stops:

Big Sur Coast offers unparalleled coastal drama. Julia Pfeiffer Burns State Park provides stunning vistas and hiking opportunities near McWay Falls.

Monterey and Carmel-by-the-Sea attractions include the Aquarium, Cannery Row, and the 17-Mile Drive loop.

Santa Cruz: The classic boardwalk, redwood climbs, and surf culture.

San Francisco: Use care while navigating the steep streets and restricted RV parking. Nearby Pacifica and Half Moon Bay provide safer basecamps.

Point Reyes National Seashore offers elk herds, lighthouse walks, and windswept seclusion.

Mendocino and Fort Bragg are cliff-hugging communities with glass beach marvels.

Avenue of the Giants: Take a parallel diversion to US-101 and travel beneath ancient redwoods.

Crescent City serves as the gateway to the Redwood National and State Parks.

RV Notes:

CA-1 north of Marin County is tiny and twisty, so take care or divert to US-101 if you're driving a big Class A.

Fuel up frequently—services become few north of Mendocino.

Fog may quickly impair vision; drive with your headlights on throughout the day.

Segment 3: Southern Oregon Coast (from Brookings to Florence)

SCAN THE QR CODE

Brookings to Florence

Distance: Approximately 160 miles.
Primary Route: US-101

Key Stops:

Pullouts along the Samuel H. Boardman Scenic Corridor provide vistas of arches, tidal pools, and cliffside walks.

Gold Beach offers Rogue River excursions and seafood shacks.

Bandon has world-class golf, seaside rock formations, and cranberry farms.

Cape Arago Loop: Discover hidden coves, tidepools, and picnic areas that are ideal for sunsets.

Florence: Sand dunes and old-town riverside charm.

RV Notes:

RV parks abound along the shore, with several offering beachfront access.

Watch for elk crossings around Brookings and Gold Beach.

Rain and wind are frequent and demand additional caution; avoid parking on coastal cliffs during storms.

Segment 4: Central and Northern Oregon Coast (Florence to Astoria)

Approximately 170 miles.
Primary Route: US-101

Key Stops:

Yachats and Cape Perpetua are known for its lava cliffs, spouting horns, and breathtaking views of the ocean.

Newport attractions include the Oregon Coast Aquarium and the Yaquina Head Lighthouse.

Lincoln City offers outlet shopping, beachcombing, and kite flying.

Tillamook Cheese Factory Tours and Dairy Land Views.

Cannon Beach has Haystack Rock and lovely craft boutiques.

Astoria: Columbia River mouth, maritime tradition, and nostalgia for The Goonies.

SCAN THE QR CODE

Florence to Astoria

RV Notes:

Beachside state parks (such as Fort Stevens and Cape Lookout) fill up fast, so reserve early.

Many of the bridges along this region are tiny and ancient; they employ care with large cargo.

Diesel gas stations are available, although steep pullouts demand downshifting in hilly areas.

Segment 5: Washington Coast (Ilwaco–Port Angeles)

SCAN THE QR CODE

Ilwaco–Port Angeles)

Approximately 200 miles.

Primary Route: US-101

Key Stops:

Long Beach Peninsula: 28 miles of open beach driving (see tide charts).

Lake Quinault offers rainforest walks and lodge-side solitude.

Kalaloch and Ruby Beach include driftwood-strewn shoreline and offshore sea stacks.

Forks: Twilight-themed tourism and scenic woodland drives.

La Push has Quileute reserve beaches and whale sightings.

Port Angeles is the launch site for Hurricane Ridge and the ferry to Victoria, British Columbia.

RV Notes:

This route is rural and difficult, with mobile service dropping in many wooded places.

Pack emergency supplies and plan for unpredictable weather in the Olympic area.

Rainforest campsites provide power connections and breathtaking privacy, but big rigs may need to establish turn radius compatibility.

Top RV Parks and Campgrounds
(Selected Highlights)

Morro Dunes RV Park in Morro Bay, California, offers walkable beach access and is a central coast center.

Ventana Campground in Big Sur, California, is located under the redwoods and has a restricted RV size.

Oceanside Beachfront RV Resort in Coos Bay, Oregon, offers elevated views of the Pacific.

Cape Lookout State Park - Oregon: Forested pathways lead to a crescent-shaped beach.

Kalaloch Campground - Washington: Perched above the seaside cliffs.

Seasonal considerations

Spring (March-May): Wildflowers along the California coast, colder temperatures in Oregon and Washington. Fewer people, but storms may continue up north.

Summer (June–August) is the peak season. Best weather, clearest sky, and the longest daylight hours. Expect fully booked parks and increased traffic density.

Fall (September-November) brings quieter roads, lush foliage in northern woods, and plenty of whale-watching chances.

Winter (December-February): Southern California stays moderate. The Oregon and Washington beaches become dramatic and stormy, perfect for gloomy photos and inside getaways.

Expert Navigation Tips

Download offline maps since cell service fails regularly in the Big Sur and Olympic Peninsula regions.

Use pullouts regularly to allow quicker vehicles to pass through winding sections.

Stay adaptable: landslides, closures, and construction are prevalent along CA-1. Detours along US-101 preserve continuity.

Check tidal charts for beach access sites, particularly in Oregon and Washington.

Hidden Gems Worth the Detour.

Elkhorn Slough (Moss Landing, California): Kayak amid otters and harbor seals.

Cape Sebastian (Gold Beach, Oregon): A lesser-known viewpoint with panoramic ocean views.

Shangri-La Trail (Port Orford, Oregon): A secluded jungle route leads to a private cove.

Soak at Sol Duc Hot Springs (WA), which is surrounded by old trees and ferns.

Final Mile

From sunny cliffs to foggy pine-lined beaches, the Pacific Coast Highway personifies the romantic ideal of the open road. For RVers, it is more than just a road; it is a rite of passage. With proper planning, a feeling of curiosity, and a flexible timetable, this tour offers stunning views, coastal food, and a newfound respect for the edge where land meets water.

Next: The Desert Southwest Loop: Red Rocks, Stargazing, and Canyon Drives from Arizona to Utah.

Route 66 (IL to CA)

SCAN THE QR CODE

"The Main Street of America"—2,448 Miles of History, Highways, and Heartland Hospitality

Overview

Route 66, which spans eight states and about 2,500 miles from Chicago's skyscrapers to the sun-kissed Santa Monica Pier, is still considered the ideal American road trip. Established in 1926 and decommissioned in 1985, the route's history lives on via protected road portions, kitschy roadside cafes, historic villages, and National Scenic Byways. RVers looking for an immersive combination of nostalgia, Americana, and ever-changing landscapes will find no better way to experience the spirit of the open road.

Quick facts.

Starting point: Chicago, Illinois.

Ending Point: Santa Monica, California

Total states: Illinois, Missouri, Kansas, Oklahoma, Texas, New Mexico, Arizona, and California.

Best travel season: April-October

Recommended duration: 2-3 weeks for the complete trip.

Fuel Planning: Frequent refueling is suggested in rural New Mexico and Arizona.

Segment Breakdown and Highlights

Illinois: Birthplace of the Mother Road (301 miles)
Key towns include Chicago, Pontiac, Bloomington, and Springfield.
Terrain: Urban start, undulating countryside, tiny town. America

Do not miss:

Route 66 Start Sign (Chicago) - Adams Street and Michigan Avenue.

Gemini Giant (Wilmington) - Towering muffler guy statue

Cozy Dog Drive-In (Springfield) is the original corn dog inventor.

Route 66 Association Hall of Fame and Museum (Pontiac).

RVer Tip: Stay overnight at Camp A While in Lincoln or Double J Campground in Chatham—both have full hookups and are RV-friendly staging areas.

Missouri: Crossroads of Culture (317 miles)
Key towns: St. Louis, Cuba, Rolla, and Springfield.
Terrain: Forested slopes, Ozark Plateau, and river crossings

Must-see stops:

Chain of Rocks Bridge - a walkable old Route 66 span over the Mississippi

Meramec Caverns, the mythical refuge of Jesse James.

Cuba's Murals: 12 full-size outdoor murals decorating historic structures.

Red's Giant Hamburg - homage to the first drive-thru

RVer Tip: Lake of the Ozarks State Park (detour option) has shaded RV sites with power hookups—a welcome respite before the long journey west.

Kansas: A Short but Sweet Stretch (13 miles)
Key towns: Galena, Riverton, and Baxter Springs.
Terrain: Rolling plains and historic mining regions.

Hidden Gems:

Cars on the Route (Galena): inspiration for Pixar's Cars characters.

Rainbow Bridge — famous single-arch concrete bridge from 1923

RVer Tip: This brief segment is easily completed in an afternoon. Park and walk around Galena's tiny historic area.

Oklahoma: Heart of Route 66 (400 miles)
Key towns include Miami, Tulsa, Oklahoma City, and Clinton.
Terrain: open plains, oil fields, prairie grasslands.

Top stops:

Blue Whale of Catoosa: roadside Americana at its best.

Route 66 Vintage Iron Motorcycle Museum, Miami

National Route 66 Museum, Elk City

Pop's 66 Soda Ranch—over 700 drinks, eye-catching neon

RVer Tip: Road conditions vary; where feasible, adhere to traditional lines. Rockwell RV Park in Oklahoma City has large sites and amenities.

Texas: A Panhandle Slice of the West (178 miles).
Key Towns: Shamrock, Amarillo
Terrain: Flatlands, big sky, ranch country

Road Icons:

U-Drop Inn (Shamrock) — Art Deco beauty became tourist center

Cadillac Ranch: 10 graffiti-covered Caddies buried snout first in the soil.

The Big Texan Steak Ranch - tackle the legendary 72oz steak challenge

RVer Tip: Palo Duro Canyon State Park, 30 minutes south of Amarillo, is a spectacular diversion with RV campsites and hiking trails.

New Mexico: The Land of Enchantment (465 miles)
Key towns: Tucumcari, Santa Rosa, Albuquerque, and Gallup.
Terrain: High desert, mesas, and adobe settlements

Cultural crossroads:

Tucumcari Tonight! has historic hotels and neon rebirth.

Blue Hole (Santa Rosa) - a spring-fed diving location

Old Town Albuquerque has adobe architecture and artisan marketplaces.

El Rancho Hotel (Gallup), a former Hollywood celebrity stopover.

RVer Tip: Be mindful about elevation increases and modulate RV brakes on downward areas. Route 66 Casino Hotel & RV Park in Albuquerque offers full-service sites.

Arizona: Painted Landscapes and Petrified Forests (401 miles).
Key towns: Holbrook, Winslow, Flagstaff, and Kingman.
Terrain: Red rock deserts, pine forests, and mountain passes.

Essential Experiences:

Petrified Forest National Park, a drive-through geological marvel.

Standing on the Corner Park (Winslow) - Eagles tribute site

Meteor Crater is one of the finest surviving impact craters.

Hackberry General Store: Route 66 time capsule.

RVer Tip: Stay overnight at Grand Canyon Railway RV Park (Williams) for easy access to Route 66 and Grand Canyon tours.

California: The Final Frontier (314 miles).

Key towns: Needles, Barstow, San Bernardino, and Santa Monica.

Terrain: Mojave Desert, mountain passes, and urban development.

Finish Strong:

Route 66 "Mother Road" Museum, Barstow

Wigwam Motel (San Bernardino): Stay in a teepee-shaped room.

Santa Monica Pier, the ceremonial terminus of Route 66.

Desert heat is strong; check radiator and tire pressure before traversing Mojave expanses. Avoid rush hour near Los Angeles to avoid stress and fuel waste.

Planning Essentials: Navigation Tips

Get offline maps and GPS tracks for retired portions.

Follow brown "Historic Route 66" markers, which vary in accuracy.

State DOT websites provide downloadable alignment maps per area.

Budget Snapshot (Per Week for Two Adults)

Expense	Estimated Cost
Fuel (diesel/gas)	$300–$500
Campground Fees	$200–$350
Food & Dining	$250–$400
Admission & Tours	100–$200
Miscellaneous	$75–$150
Total	**$925–$1,600**

RV Park Pro Picks

Double J Campground (IL)

Route 66 KOA (OKC, Oklahoma)

Amarillo Ranch RV Park (Texas)

Enchanted Trails RV Park (NM)

Railside RV Ranch (Az)

Desert View RV Resort (Ca)

Final Word

Route 66 is more than just a line on a map; it's a living museum of

America's history, replete with tales, people, and long-forgotten achievements. Whether you travel the full route or just a few sections, each mile tells a tale of national history, highlighted by roadside neon, dusty landscapes, and timeworn communities. RVers consider it a rite of passage that should be done gently, with eyes wide open and tanks full.

Blue Ridge Parkway (VA to NC)

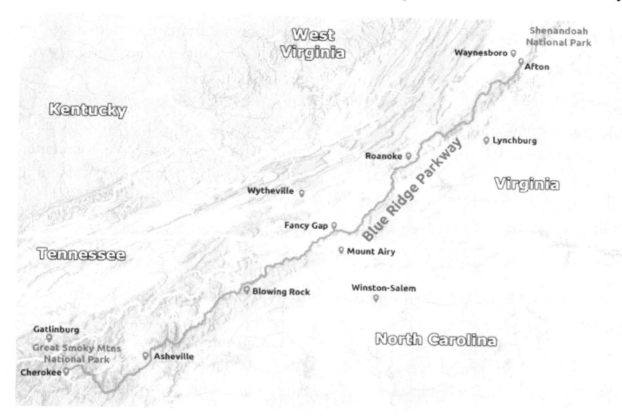

America's Favorite Drive: A Rolling Symphony of Scenic Wonders.

Overview

The Blue Ridge Parkway, which stretches 469 miles from the foggy ridgelines of Shenandoah National Park in Virginia to the highland core of Great Smoky Mountains National Park in North Carolina, is more than a road; it's a tailored experience. This historic byway connects two national parks by a ribbon of asphalt stretched across the Appalachian highlands, offering a painting of shifting heights, cultural diversity, and panoramic mountain views.

The parkway, designed in the 1930s with motorists in mind, is remarkable in that it has no commercial vehicles, no advertising, and a design speed restriction that seldom exceeds 45 mph. What's the goal? To urge visitors to slow down and appreciate the beauty. For RVers, it provides a unique combination of natural immersion, well-placed campsites, and pull-offs designed to maximize panoramic vistas.

Quick facts: Length: 469 miles.

Termini: Shenandoah National Park, Virginia (Milepost 0), to Great Smoky Mountains National Park, North Carolina (Milepost 469).

Best season: mid-April to late October (fall foliage peaks mid-October).

Speed limit: 25–45 mph (strictly enforced)

RV Access: Fully accessible to RVs under 45 feet in total length; exercise care on tight turns.

Cell coverage is spotty; download offline maps.

Tunnels: 26 (mainly in NC; see height limits)

Route breakdown per region.
Virginia Highlands (MilePost 0-150)
Begin at Rockfish Gap, just south of Waynesboro, VA, where the parkway extends from Skyline Drive. This region is dominated by rolling countryside and modest peaks.

Highlights:

Humpback Rocks (MP 5.8): Traditional mountain farm display and a short but steep trek with breathtaking views.

Peaks of Otter (MP 86): A classic stop with a campsite, visitor center, and access to Sharp Top's summit trail.

James River (MP 63.6): Lowest elevation point; take a walk down the river to learn about the canal period.

Campgrounds: Otter Creek and Peaks of Otter have RV-friendly sites with no connections but potable water and dump facilities.

The Plateau Region (Milepost 150-275) represents the cultural center of the Appalachians. Expect a mix of woodland hills and expansive farming plateaus. This area is dotted with handmade businesses, old-time music venues, and picturesque vistas.

Highlights:

Mabry Mill (MP 176.1) is one of the parkway's most photographed locations; don't miss the living history displays.

Blue Ridge Music Center (MP 213) celebrates Appalachian music tradition; schedule your visit around a live performance.

Rocky Knob (MP 167.1) provides access to the Rock Castle Gorge Trail and RV sites.

RV Tips: This portion has softer turns and broader roadways, making it ideal for bigger rigs. Use authorized turnouts to enjoy the views.

High Country (mileposts 275–340)
The topography tightens as the parkway passes through higher heights and difficult terrain around Boone and Blowing Rock. The weather here varies fast, so check predictions before heading out.

Highlights:

Linn Cove Viaduct (MP 304): An engineering masterpiece that hugs Grandfather Mountain; explore the visitor center path underneath.

Julian Price Memorial Park (MP 297) is a 4,200-acre recreational refuge that offers lake kayaking, hiking, and RV camping.

Moses H. Cone Memorial Park (MP 294.1) has carriage routes, a crafts center, and a manor home surrounded by meadows.

Tunnel Alert: Tunnels become increasingly common south of MP 300; the minimum clearance is 10'6" at Pine Mountain Tunnel (MP 399.1). RVs longer than 11 feet should travel with care or consider other routes.

Pisgah Highlands (mileposts 340–469)
This section takes you into the high country of Western North Carolina, where altitudes rise and biodiversity thrives. The Blue Ridge Parkway reaches its highest point at slightly over 6,000 feet.

Highlights:

Craggy Gardens (MP 364.6): Rhododendrons bloom in late spring; hike for panoramic ridge views.

Mount Mitchell State Park (access at MP 355.4) is the highest point east of the Mississippi, with a driveable summit and excellent trails.

Pisgah Inn (MP 408.6): One of the few places on the parkway that provides both dining and overnight accommodations.

Waterrock Knob (MP 451.2): Near the southern terminus, this overlook provides expansive views and a steep but rewarding trail.

Mount Pisgah Campground can accommodate RVs up to 40 feet with some electric hookups. Limited generator hours apply—ideal for peaceful mountain evenings.

Navigation & Safety

Mapping: Milepost markers appear every 0.2 to 0.5 miles and are essential for orientation, especially when GPS fails.

Fuel: There are no gas stations directly along the parkway. Plan refueling stops in nearby towns such as Boone, Floyd, and Asheville.

Winter Closures: Portions are closed due to snow and ice, particularly above 3,500 feet. The NPS Blue Ridge Parkway road conditions map provides real-time closure information.

Drive Times: Allow at least 3-4 days for the entire route. Some RVers take 7-10 days to fully appreciate their journey.

Hidden Gems and Off the Beaten Path

Roanoke Mountain Loop (MP 120.3): Scenic spur road ideal for smaller RVs.

Doughton Park (MP 241.1): Less busy trails and ranger-led activities.

Little Switzerland (Exit MP 334): A lovely alpine community right off the parkway with gem mining and quaint inns.

Practical RV Tips

RVs Over 35 ft: Manageable throughout, however sharper switchbacks from MP 320–420 may demand care and lower speed.

Boondocking: Not authorized on the parkway itself, although several surrounding National Forest properties provide scattered camping.

Reservations: Campgrounds along the parkway fill rapidly during peak leaf season—book early at Recreation.gov.

Budget Snapshot (7-Day Itinerary Example for Two)

Category	Estimated Cost
Fuel (round trip)	$150–$250
Campsites	$140–$210
Groceries/Supplies	$100–$150
Park Fees	$0 (no entry fee)
Attractions	$50–$100
Total	**$440–$710**

Final Mile Thoughts

The Blue Ridge Parkway is more than just a route; it's a national treasure designed for leisure, not rush. With each mile, it offers a new layer of Appalachian beauty: hand-hewn traditions, cloud-kissed peaks, and views that seem to stop time. For the RVer, it's more than simply a destination; it's a wonderful trip experience.

Great River Road (MN to LA)

SCAN THE QR CODE

Route Overview

The Great River Road is a designated National Scenic Byway that follows the Mississippi River's meandering journey for over 3,000 miles, from its headwaters at Lake Itasca in Minnesota to the Gulf of Mexico in Louisiana. This renowned route, which passes through 10 states and innumerable river towns, takes you on an immersive trip into the heart of the country, rich in natural beauty, cultural legacy, and historical importance. The Great River Road is ideal for RV travelers looking for a mix of small-town charm, ecological beauty, and classic Americana. It's both a big adventure and a deep dive into America's varied ecosystem.

Route Snapshot

Total distance: around 3,000 miles.

States visited include Minnesota, Wisconsin, Iowa, Illinois, Missouri, Kentucky, Tennessee, Arkansas, Mississippi, and Louisiana.

Estimated duration: 3-5 weeks (adjustable depending on stops and diversions).

The best time to go is between May and October.

Road Conditions: Mostly state highways and county roads; paved and well-maintained, with occasional rural diversions.

Minnesota's northern origins and headwaters begin in Lake Itasca State Park.

Highlight: Cross the Mississippi River at its source.

Must-see attractions include Bemidji's Paul Bunyan and Babe sculptures, Grand Rapids' Forest History Center, and the ancient village of Winona, with its river bluffs.

RV Tips: There are plenty of roomy state campsites with power connections; keep an eye out for deer after nightfall.

Wisconsin: Bluffs and Backroads.
Key Towns: La Crosse and Prairie du Chien

Scenic feature: The river is surrounded by spectacular limestone cliffs.

Experience the Driftless Area's splendor, Native American effigy mounds at Effigy Mounds National Monument (just over the border in Iowa), and rolling countryside studded with dairy farms.

Local flavors include cheese curds, cranberry festivals in the autumn, and traditional dinner clubs.

Iowa: Americana on the River Notable towns include Dubuque and Davenport.

Don't miss Dubuque's National Mississippi River Museum & Aquarium, as well as the Quad Cities' waterfront bike paths.

RV Friendly: Numerous county parks, historic riverside campsites, and reasonably priced city-owned RV spots with full hookups.

Illinois: Mark Twain Country and Industrial Legacy.
Cultural Crossroads: Galena (preserved nineteenth-century town), Nauvoo (Mormon and pioneer history), and Alton (haunted tales and limestone cliffs).

Drive Highlights: The route avoids industrial centers while yet providing access to beautiful communities and peaceful natural areas.

Insider Tip: The Chain of Rocks Bridge provides pedestrian access and a stunning perspective of the Mississippi.

Missouri: Where the Rivers Meet.
Major hub: St. Louis.

Landmark: Gateway Arch National Park; ride the tram to the top for panoramic views.

Southbound Gems: Ste. Genevieve's French Colonial quarter, and Cape Girardeau's river paintings.

Navigation Alert: Interchanges near St. Louis may be crowded; plan your crossing during off-peak hours.

Kentucky: River Bends and Quiet Detours.
Short yet scenic: The Great River Road enters Kentucky at Wickliffe.

Historic Sites: Wickliffe Mounds State Historic Site — ancient Mississippian culture.

RV Stay: Columbus-Belmont State Park has covered areas with river views.

Tennessee: Soulful Stopovers.
Cultural Pulse: Memphis.

Must-See: Blues, BBQ, and Beale Street; Sun Studio and Graceland for music history enthusiasts.

Overnight Options: The Memphis region has commercial RV campgrounds and dump stations, so plan ahead for peak music events.

Arkansas' visual palette features open skies, flat delta landscapes, and cotton heritage.

Points of interest include Helena-West Helena's King Biscuit Blues Festival (October), the Delta Cultural Center, and picturesque levee drives.

Driving Tip: Through farmland zones, keep your speed down because roads might be narrow and without shoulders.

Mississippi: River Lore & Southern Elegance

Historic anchors include Natchez and Vicksburg.

Explore antebellum homes, Civil War battlefields, and steamboat history.

Nature Detour: Take a side excursion along the Natchez Trace Parkway for a peaceful parallel path with less commercial activity.

RV Advisory: Keep an eye on river stages during storm season; campsites along the river may flood briefly.

Louisiana: River to Gulf
Final stretch: Baton Rouge to Venice.

Must-see destinations include Baton Rouge's Old State Capitol, New Orleans' bustling French Quarter, and the last river meanders near Plaquemines Parish.

Southern cuisine: fresh beignets, po'boys, and crawfish boils.

RV Access: New Orleans has many RV resorts with shuttle service to downtown; nevertheless, be cautious of tight city traffic.

Navigation and Planning Essentials

Route Markers: Look for green pilot wheel markers indicating the Great River Road in each state.

Mobile Tools: The "MRPC Great River Road" app offers state-by-state GPS-based advice, sites of interest, and detour notifications.

Bridge crossings: There are several options, and certain bridges provide particularly attractive vantage views, notably around Memphis, Dubuque, and Baton Rouge.

Budget Breakdown:

gasoline (Full Route): $1,200-$2,000 (depending on RV type and average gasoline cost of $4 per gallon).

Campsites (30 nights): $600-$1,200 (a mix of public and private RV parks)

Attractions and Museums: $200–$400.

Dining and supplies: $800 to $1,500.

Highlights Map (Quick Reference)

● Minnesota locations include Lake Itasca, Grand Rapids, and Winona. Wisconsin: La Crosse and Prairie du Chien.
● Iowa: Dubuque and Davenport.
● Illinois: Galena and Alton
● Missouri: St. Louis, Ste. Genevieve. Kentucky: Wickliffe. Tennessee: Memphis.
● Arkansas: Helena, Delta Scenic Byway.
● Mississippi: Vicksburg and Natchez.
● Louisiana includes Baton Rouge, New Orleans, and Venice.

Final Word:

The Great River Road is more than simply a highway; it's a ribbon that connects America's business, culture, conflict, and communities. From Minnesota's whispering forests to Louisiana's moss-draped bayous, this epic trip rewards patience, curiosity, and the spirit of travel. Bring a comprehensive road map, maintain your gasoline tank above half, and make room in your schedule for the unplanned—because some of the nicest portions of the Great River Road can't be found in guidebooks.

The Loneliest Road (US-50)

Overview:

US-50, which runs from Ocean City, Maryland to Sacramento, California, is a transcontinental ribbon of roadway that cuts across the United States with a sense of rebellion and loneliness. However, it is the Nevada section—more than 400 miles of harsh, sweeping desert—that gave the route its legendary name: The Loneliest Road in America. Despite the name, this famed path offers everything but nothingness. US-50 is rich in history, geological marvel, and untouched vistas, and it rewards the prepared RV traveler with a journey that is both contemplative and breathtaking.

This corridor is not about speed or spectacle; rather, it is about perseverance, discovery, and reconnecting with the raw, vast landscapes of the American West. Proper preparation is required, since fuel stops are few, cell service is patchy, and weather may be unexpected. However, for those who want freedom and raw beauty, this journey is the pinnacle of solo road trips.

Route Summary:
Total length: around 3,073 miles.
Key Segment Focus: Ely, Nevada to Fallon, Nevada (the "loneliest" part - around 300 miles)
States covered: Maryland, District of Columbia, Virginia, West Virginia, Ohio, Indiana, Illinois, Missouri, Kansas, Colorado, Utah, Nevada, and California.
Primary terrain includes desert basins, mountain ranges, broad plains, and rolling farms.

Essential Navigation and Planning Tips
Fuel Strategy: Fill up before leaving Ely or Fallon. The only major gasoline stations along the Nevada route are in Ely, Eureka, Austin, and Fallon. When traveling in rural areas, bring additional gasoline or an auxiliary tank.

Water Supply: Because this road passes through dry areas, it requires enough drinkable water. A minimum of one gallon per person per day is recommended, plus reserves.

Maintenance Prepare: Make sure your tires are in excellent condition (including your spare). Bring coolant, extra oil, and a tool kit. Some parts are more than 100 kilometers long without any services.

Connectivity: Cell service is patchy at best. Download offline maps and bring a paper atlas or a preloaded GPS device. Satellite messengers are recommended for lengthy off-grid travel.

RV Compatibility: Suitable for all classes, however longer Class A and towed trailers should exercise caution on certain tight corners and high mountain passes in the Utah-Nevada transition zones.

Featured Stops and Sites Along the Loneliest Corridor

Ely, Nevada
Altitude: 6,437 feet.
Ely, a historic copper mining boomtown, today serves as the entrance to Great Basin experiences. Before driving west, stop at the Nevada Northern Railway Museum, which offers vintage steam train excursions, and fill up on supplies in the area. The neighboring Ward Charcoal Ovens State Historic Park offers an insight into 19th-century industry and has RV parks.

Great Basin National Park

A short detour south from US-50 via NV-487 and NV-488. Highlights include Lehman Caves, Wheeler Peak Scenic Drive, and some of the darkest night sky in the continental United States, perfect for astronomy. Several parks can accommodate RVs up to 35 feet.

Eureka, Nevada

Population: ~500.
Eureka, nicknamed the "Friendliest Town on the Loneliest Road," is home to a renovated 19th-century opera theater, a quaint historical museum, and petrol stations. The streets are walking, and there is RV parking downtown.

Austin, Nevada

Austin, located at 6,605 feet, feels like a high-altitude time capsule. The architecture and abandoned silver mills bear witness to mining history. Explore Stokes Castle, a three-story stone tower with magnificent views. There is little gasoline and food available, so prepare appropriately.

Middlegate Station

This former Pony Express station is a one-building village that serves hefty burgers, ice-cold beverages, and tales from the furthest reaches of the desert. It's an ambient pit break with primitive RV overnight parking (no hookups).

Sandy Mountain Recreation Area

This 600-foot-tall singing sand dune, located just east of Fallon, is a popular destination for off-roaders and geology aficionados. Camping is permitted in dispersed areas with no services other than vault toilets. Low-clearance RVs and trailers should remain on the main gravel route.

Fallon, Nevada

Population: around 9,000.
The western bookend of the Loneliest Road's renowned segment. Fallon, home to the Naval Air Station, Lattin Farms, and the Oats Park Art Center, also has full-service RV parks, repair shops, and supermarkets, which are a pleasant respite after miles of desert seclusion.

Camping and Overnight Options

Locati on	Type	Hooku ps	Notes
			ough sites

Locati on	Type	Hooku ps	Notes
Ely KOA Journe y	RV Park	Full	Dog park, Wi-Fi, propan e
Great Basin NP – Lower Lehma n Creek	Nation al Park	Dry	First-c ome, first-se rved
Eureka RV Park	City Park	Water/ Electri c	Basic ameniti es, walk to town
Bob Scott Campg round (Austin)	Nation al Forest	Dry	Shaded , scenic, quiet
Middle gate Station	Dispers ed	None	Rustic, free overnig ht with meal purcha se
Fallon RV Park	Comm ercial	Full	Laundr y, pull-thr

Seasonal considerations

Spring (April-May): Higher altitudes may still have snow, so keep an eye out for abrupt temperature decreases. Ideal for cool, crowd-free travel.

Summer (June–August): Expect triple-digit temperatures in basins. Begin early and rest midday. Carry extra coolant and pay strict attention to tire pressure.

Autumn (September-October) is ideal for seeing color changes in mountain passes and enjoying temperate weather. Stargazing is at its height.

Winter (November–March): Snow and ice are likely, particularly around Ely and Great Basin National Park. Many campsites are closed; check circumstances before leaving.

Wildlife and Caution Zones

Open Range Grazing: Cattle wander freely over Nevada's roadway. Drive carefully, particularly at night.

Desert wildlife includes antelope, jackrabbits, coyotes, and wild horses. Keep food sealed and pets secure at campgrounds.

Wind gusts between valleys and mountain passes may have a significant influence on big RVs. Use lower speeds and keep both hands on the wheel.

Why Travel the Loneliest Road?

To follow US-50 through Nevada is to embark on one of the most unusual American journeys—a test of self-reliance on a route few dare to travel. It's both a spiritual detox and a study of stark geography. There are no diversions for the impatient, nor is there a shoulder for hesitating. Just the wide road, the rhythmic hum of tires on sun-kissed asphalt, and the steady unfolding of an untamed chapter in the American landscape.

Whether as a piece of a cross-country itinerary or the heart of your western trip, US-50 is more than a route; it's a rite of passage for the RV traveler looking for something meaningful beyond the map.

Note: US-50 signs may be irregular. Always use up-to-date GPS data and state highway maps. Many turnouts and scenic landmarks go unmarked; keep a lookout for modest brown signs and historical plaques hidden off the shoulder.

Next Atlas entry: US-93: The Great Basin Highway - From Borderlands to Basin, Experience Nevada's Quiet Majesty.

Alaska Highway (Dawson Creek to Fairbanks)

SCAN THE QR CODE

Distance: approximately 1,390 miles (2,237 kilometers) Best travel season: Late May to early September.

Route: Dawson Creek, BC to Fort Nelson, Watson Lake, Whitehorse, Tok, Delta Junction, and Fairbanks, AK.

Overview

The Alaska Highway, which began as a military supply route during World War II and later became a legendary overland route into the Last Frontier, is more than just a road; it is an odyssey. This epic transnational corridor begins in Dawson Creek, British Columbia (Mile 0) and travels through remote boreal forests, sweeping mountain ranges, and vast tundra before ending in Fairbanks, Alaska. Whether you're looking for wildlife, peace, or the wild sounds of untamed land, this is where rubber meets rugged adventure.

SCAN THE QR CODE

Dawson Creek to Fort Nelson

Key Highlights by Segment

Dawson Creek to Fort Nelson (Mile 0–283)

The terrain is rolling farmland that transitions into thick northern woods.

Do not miss:

Mile 0 Post in Dawson Creek is a symbolic photo stop.

Kiskatinaw Bridge (Mile 21) is a rare curved wooden trestle bridge built in 1942.

Fort St. John is your last major stop for RV supplies until Fort Nelson.

Fuel Tip: Fill up in Fort St. John; stations become scarce and expensive north of here.

Fort Nelson to Watson Lake (Miles 283 to 635)
Terrain: Winding climbs through the Northern Rockies, with wildlife-rich valleys.

Wildlife Hotspot: Moose, black bears, bison, caribou – especially near Muncho Lake.

Scenic Gem:

Muncho Lake Provincial Park - turquoise glacial waters, great for boondocking with a view.

Liard River Hot Springs (Mile 497) — bathe in warm, mineral-rich waters among boreal wilderness.

Road Conditions: Steep hills and turns; slower speeds suggested for RVers.

Watson Lake to Whitehorse (Mile 635 to Mile 918)

Terrain: Rolling hills and flowing river valleys.

Signature Stop:

Watson Lake Sign Post Forest - approximately 100,000 signs; bring your own to add to the collection.

SCAN THE QR CODE

Fort Nelson to Watson Lake

Teslin Bridge (Mile 804) — ancient cantilever bridge spanning the Teslin River.

Whitehorse: Largest city in Yukon; complete RV service facilities, groceries, laundry, and mechanics.

Visit the SS Klondike sternwheeler, or explore Miles Canyon for walks with canyon vistas.

Whitehorse to Tok (Mile 918 to Mile 1,237)

Terrain: Remote wilderness with infrequent habitation.

Border Crossing: U.S. Customs at Port Alcan; valid passports and car registration needed.

Points of Interest:

Kluane National Park - glaciers, grizzlies, and Canada's highest peak (Mount Logan).

Destruction Bay and Burwash Landing are quiet lakeside stops with pull-through RV sites.

Keep an eye out for frost heaves and construction zones, and drive slowly in such places.

Tok to Fairbanks (Miles 1,237–1,390)

Terrain: Gentle hills that transition into boreal flatlands.

Welcome to Alaska. Tok is the state's first main center, known as "Main Street" Alaska.

Final Stretch:

Delta Junction (Mile 1,360) marks the official conclusion of the Alaska Highway.

Fairbanks is a full-service city that provides fuel, groceries, RV parks, and access to the Dalton Highway for those traveling north to the Arctic Circle.

Navigation Notes

Road Conditions: Fully paved, but weathered; potholes, frost heaves, and gravel stretches are common.

Speed limits vary by province and state, but are usually between 50 and 65 mph (80 and 105 km/h); pay attention to signs.

Cell Coverage: Expect extended dead zones; bring a satellite phone or GPS beacon in an emergency.

Wildlife Caution: Animals regularly cross without notice, particularly around dawn and twilight.

RV Essentials Checklist

Spare Tires and Tools: Sharp gravel and debris frequently cause punctures.

Water and Propane Reserves: Services may be closed or hours reduced during shoulder seasons.

Maps & Milepost Guide: While GPS is useful, a physical mile-by-mile guide is still essential.

Top Campgrounds & Boondocking Sites

Location	Campground	Hookups	Notes
Muncho Lake	Northern Rockies Lodge	Partial	Stunning lakefront RV sites.
Whitehorse	Hi Country RV Park	Full	Laundry, Wi-Fi, and large pull-thr

			oughs.
Tok	Tok RV Village	Full	Dump station, gas, propane, and restocking.
Delta Junction	Quartz Lake SP	Dry	Quiet lakeside camping near the highway.

			parks.
Food	$30/day	$60/day	Groceries are more expensive north of Whitehorse.
Activities	Mostly free	Some guided tours	Hot springs, museums, parks.

Budget Snapshot

Category	Low-End	Mid-Range	Notes
Fuel (Round Trip)	$800	1,200+	Based on ~8 mpg RV fuel economy.
Campgrounds	$25/night	$50/night	Mix of dry camping and full-service

Seasonal Advice

The best time to go is from late May to early September. Snowfall may happen even in June.

Mosquito season is June and July; pack powerful repellant and protected enclosures.

Fire Season: July and August—check wildfire notifications and air quality before going out.

Final Notes

This is not a path for rushing. The Alaska Highway encourages cautious pace, silent observation, and flexibility. The route may surprise you—mudslides, roaming moose, washed-out bridges—but each turn offers magnificence unparalleled in North America. Prepare wisely, drive carefully, and you'll be rewarded with an experience that exemplifies RVing at its most fundamental and remarkable.

Chapter 4: Regional RV Adventures

Northeast:

New England Fall Foliage Loop

Overview

The New England Fall Foliage Loop is one of the most famous RV travels in the United States, a yearly pilgrimage timed to coincide with nature's most vibrant display. This circular route passes through six states—Connecticut, Rhode Island, Massachusetts, Vermont, New Hampshire, and Maine—each with a rich tapestry of hues, historical charm, and small-town warmth. The 900-mile trek is best completed between late September and mid-October, when sugar maples illuminate the countryside in shades of scarlet, gold, and burnt orange.

This road is more than just a scenic drive; it's a moving painting of historical towns, covered bridges, antique byways, and wooded mountain passes. Designed exclusively for RVers, this book explains the best routes, overnight breaks, spectacular overlooks, and practical recommendations to make the most of your fall adventure.

Route Summary Total distance: around 950 miles.

Recommended Duration: 10–14 days

Ideal Travel window: Late September until mid-October.

Start/End Point: Hartford, Connecticut (loop)

SCAN THE QR CODE

New England

Route Breakdown and Key Stops
1. Connecticut: Gateway to the Loop (start point - about 75 miles)
Route: Hartford to Litchfield Hills to Mystic. Highlights:

Route 7 through Litchfield County is a meandering route lined with stone walls, white steeples, and golden canopies.

Kent Falls State Park: A short climb rewards with flowing waterfalls and lush greenery.

Mystic Seaport: Coastal attractiveness meets maritime heritage—a peaceful contrast to the interior surroundings.

RV Notes:

RV parks abound around Torrington and Mystic.

Low-clearance warnings on older municipal roads; verify GPS height requirements.

2. Rhode Island: Coastal Colors (about 55 miles)
Main Route: Westerly to Newport.
Highlights:

Ocean Drive in Newport: A coastal combination of thundering surf and bright tree lines—rarely crowded during the shoulder season.

Newport Mansions: Gilded Age buildings surrounded by blazing flora, best seen from Cliff Walk.

There is limited RV access inside Newport proper; on weekends, utilize satellite parking with shuttle service.

Fishermen's Memorial State Park has full hookups and is close to coastal attractions.

3. Massachusetts: Colonial Roads and Mountain Passes (~150 miles)
Main Route: Cape Ann - Concord - Berkshires Highlights:

Mohawk Trail (Route 2): One of America's oldest scenic byways, particularly beautiful from Shelburne Falls to North Adams.

The Berkshires are home to October's golden crescendo. Visit Mount Greylock for magnificent views that extend into Vermont.

Scenic detours:

Route 112 is quiet and less crowded, making it excellent for leaf peeping away from the major highways.

RV Notes:

The Berkshires are ideal for RV travelers; select campsites around Pittsfield or North Adams for easy access to trailheads and cultural attractions.

4. Crimson Kingdom, Vermont (about 175 miles).
Main Route: Bennington, Manchester, Stowe, and Northeast Kingdom.
Highlights:

Smugglers' Notch (Route 108): Follow a winding route through a beautiful mountain pass surrounded by lush greenery.

Stowe: The quintessential autumn village, with a historic church tower perched near Mount Mansfield.

Northeast Kingdom: Remote, rough, and less traveled—a paradise for dedicated nature lovers.

Scenic overlooks:

On clear days, Hogback Mountain (Route 9) offers vistas of up to 100 miles.

Moss Glen Falls: A little roadside stroll with a great result near Granville.

RV Notes:

Narrow mountain roads need caution while driving heavier vehicles.

If you want to drive far into the Kingdom area, consider smaller Class B or tow-behind vehicles.

Water and garbage stations are rare in isolated northern areas; prepare appropriately.

5. Granite Peaks and Fiery Forests in New Hampshire (~150 miles)
Main Route: White Mountains Loop (Kancamagus Highway, Franconia Notch, Mt. Washington Valley).
Highlights:

Kancamagus Highway (Route 112): A 34.5-mile stretch through the White Mountain National Forest, probably the pinnacle of autumn foliage drives.

Mount Washington Auto Road: Drive or join a guided trip to see high-altitude vistas ranging from gold to crimson to alpine tundra.

Franconia Notch State Park: For a close-up view of the foliage, hike Flume Gorge or ride the multi-use route.

RV Notes:

Kancamagus features designated RV-friendly pull-offs and campsites; no hookups—dry camping is required.

Fall weekends are high traffic days; arrive early for the greatest parking and picture opportunities.

6. Maine's lakes, forests, and coastlines span around 250 miles.
Highlights along the main route include Sebago Lake, Rangeley Lakes, and Acadia National Park.

Rangeley Lakes Scenic Byway: Reflections of fire-hued maples glisten in quiet water.

Acadia National Park: Combine autumn hues with breaking Atlantic waves by visiting Jordan Pond and Cadillac Mountain at dawn.

Camden Hills State Park: View Penobscot Bay via a curtain of fall color.

RV Notes:

RVs are permitted in Acadia's Blackwoods and Seawall campsites, subject to some limitations; book early.

Avoid driving heavy trucks down tiny downtown Bar Harbor streets and instead use park-and-ride areas.

Loop Return: Maine → New Hampshire → Massachusetts → Connecticut (approx. 150 miles).
Complete the round by taking Route 302 via Conway, NH, then I-91 southbound through Massachusetts back to Hartford. Finally, visit Yankee Candle Village in Deerfield, a fall-themed shopping experience with a local flair.

Best Scenic Byways for RVs

Byway	State	Length	Notes
Kancamagus Highway	NH	34.5 mi	No services, but large turnouts and parking
Mohawk Trail	MA	63 mi	Steep grades; watch engine braking
Rangeley Lakes Byway	ME	35 mi	Low traffic, expansive lake

			views
Route 100	VT	216 mi	Full north-south traverse of Vermont's spine
Route 7	CT	78 mi	Classic stone-wall-lined drive

Timing your trip by region. Peak foliage dates

Region	Peak Foliage Date
Northern Maine	Late Sept – Early Oct
White Mountains, NH	Early – Mid Oct
Green Mountains, VT	Early – Mid Oct
Massachusetts & Rhode Island	Mid – Late Oct
Connecticut Mid	Late Oct

Essential Tips for RVers

Book early: Peak foliage corresponds with high camping demand, so book state parks and private sites 3-6 months in advance.

Weather Watch: Autumn weather in New England is unpredictable. Prepare for cool mornings, warm afternoons, and unexpected rain.

Height Matters: Some historic towns and picturesque highways have low-clearance bridges or weight limits. Use RV-specific GPS applications.

Travel Midweek: Plan your travel between Tuesday and Thursday to avoid weekend traffic and crowded outlooks.

Slow Down: With narrow roads, abrupt twists, and gorgeous diversions, a slower speed is both safer and more pleasurable.

Final Thoughts

The New England Fall Foliage Loop is more than just a drive; it's a specially planned trip through America's historic heartland beneath a canopy of color. From Maine's seaside cliffs to Vermont's maple-covered hills, this path offers opportunities for adventure at every turn. RVers who drive wisely and keep flexible may enjoy one of the natural world's most spectacular seasonal displays—engine idling low, camera in hand, and the road ahead painted in flame.

Adirondacks & Finger Lakes

SCAN THE QR CODE

Overview

The vast wilderness of the Adirondack Mountains and the calm, glacier-carved valleys of the Finger Lakes are where New York's wild heart pulses the most strongly. This area, connected by gorgeous byways, quaint towns, and a strong sense of outdoor adventure, is ideal for RV travelers wanting both rugged isolation and small-town welcome.

The Adirondack Park is the biggest publicly protected region in the contiguous United States, covering over six million acres—more than Yellowstone, Everglades, Glacier, and Grand Canyon National Parks combined. To the west, the Finger Lakes create a necklace of long, narrow lakes nestled among rolling farmland and lush woodland, with wineries, waterfalls, and historic sites thriving at every turn of the route.

Major RV Routes.

Adirondack Trail Scenic Byway (NY-30).
Distance: around 170 miles.

Route: Malone to Fonda.

Highlights include Tupper Lake, Long Lake, Blue Mountain Lake, and Speculator.

Ideal RV Class: All classes, but anticipate tight portions in hilly areas.

This byway cuts across the Adirondack backcountry, along wooded ridgelines and lakefront townships. Don't miss The Wild Center near Tupper Lake, which offers treetop treks and immersive environmental displays. Blue Mountain Lake is a scenic destination, featuring the Adirondack Experience museum highlighting area history.

Central Adirondack Trail (NY-28).
Distance: around 140 miles.

Route: North Creek to Old Forge.

Highlights: Raquette Lake, Inlet, and Adirondack Scenic Railroad.

Travel Tip: Avoid peak leaf-peeping weekends for easier navigation.

NY-28 passes through postcard-perfect villages and good hiking scenery. The road provides convenient access to campers with lakeside views and several trailheads into the High Peaks region. Raquette Lake excursions provide a taste of Gilded Age luxury among the woodland majesty.

The Finger Lakes Wine Country Loop spans approximately 200 miles.

Route: Canandaigua to Seneca Lake, then to Keuka Lake, Watkins Glen, Ithaca, and finally to Skaneateles.

Surface: Smoothly paved roads with enough shoulder width

Driving Season: Best from May to October.

This loop is a leisurely tour of New York's viticulture corridor, including stops at Riesling tastings, farm markets, and artisan cheese stores. RV-friendly wineries such as Three Brothers, Fox Run, and Dr. Konstantin Frank provide ample parking and even overnight accommodations. With 19 cascading waterfalls and stunning canyon paths, Watkins Glen serves as the route's anchor point.

Notable campgrounds

Lake George RV Park is located in Lake George, New York.

Open: April to October.

Amenities include full hookups, on-site trolleys, biking paths, and an indoor pool

Insider Tip: Make reservations months in advance on summer weekends.

A full-service resort-style park ideal for family vacations in the southern Adirondacks. It gives fast access to boating, shopping, and traditional amusement parks like The Great Escape.

Jellystone Park at North Hudson
Location: Between Schroon Lake and Elizabethtown

Open: May–October.

Best For: Families with kids; themed weekends and playgrounds

A festive entryway to the High Peaks area, complete with full-service facilities. Ideal for those going to visit Mount Marcy, New York's highest peak.

Clute Park Campground in Watkins Glen, NY

Open: April to October.

Type: Municipal campsite with electricity and water.

Distance to Watkins Glen State Park: 0.5 kilometers.

Popular with RVers visiting the Finger Lakes Wine Festival or activities at Watkins Glen International Raceway.

Top Attractions for RVers

Adirondack High Peaks Access Points: Keene Valley, Lake Placid

RV parking is limited near trailheads; explore shuttle services or park-and-hike possibilities.

Recommended Hikes: Cascade Mountain (moderate) and Mount Jo (easy).

Saranac Lake & Lake Placid

Lake Placid, which hosted the Winter Olympics in 1932 and 1980, is today a popular destination for mountain sports, museums, and lakeside strolls. Visit the Olympic Jumping Complex, or kayak Mirror Lake.

Taughannock Falls State Park

This park in Trumansburg has a 215-foot waterfall, which is taller than Niagara Falls. Paved RV parking and power hookups are provided. Level pathways make this an ideal visit for families or people with restricted mobility.

Corning Museum of Glass

Located just south of the Finger Lakes, the museum has interactive displays and live glassblowing. There is enough RV parking on site.

Navigation Tips

Mountain Roads: Be cautious on switchbacks and elevation climbs in the Adirondacks—downshift early and brake lightly to minimize overheating.

Cell service is patchy in the Adirondack interior; plan ahead of time by downloading maps and campsite information.

Fuel stops are limited along NY-30 and NY-28; fill tanks in communities such as Ticonderoga, Saranac Lake, and Old Forge.

Weather Watch: Sudden storms are typical at high heights; always check the forecast before driving in the mountains.

Best Travel Seasons

Spring (May-June): Waterfalls peak in the Finger Lakes, while wildflowers blanket the forest floor.

Summer (July to August): Full camping services and lake fun. Reservations must be made in advance.

Fall (late September to mid October): Both locations have world-class foliage; nevertheless, expect more traffic and limited camping availability.

Winter: Limited RV access; ideal for experienced winter campers or those near ski resorts such as Whiteface.

Budget Snapshot (per day for two people in a Class-C RV)

Expense Type	Adirondacks ($)	Finger Lakes ($)
RV Site (w/full hook-up)	40–80	35–75
Fuel (regional driving)	25–40	20–35
Attractions & Tours	15–50	10–40
Groceries/ Dining	30–60	30–60
Winery Visits/Tastings	—	10–25 (per stop)

Professional Tips for a Smooth Journey

RV-Friendly Wineries: Look for "Harvest Hosts" where you may stay overnight following tastings.

Dump stations may be found at most state parks and welcome centers; see the New York DEC website for particular locations.

State statutes prohibit moving firewood more than 50 kilometers to avoid the spread of invasive pests. Purchase locally.

Water Refills: Reliable spigots are accessible in DEC campsites, service plazas, and most state parks.

Essential Stops at a Glance

Stop	Region	Must-See	Recommended Time
Lake Placid	Adirondacks	Olympic Museum, Mirror Lake	Half-day to full day
Watkins Glen	Finger Lakes	Gorge Trail, Seneca Lake	1–2 days
Tupper	Adiron	The	Half-da

Lake	dacks	Wild Center, Skywalk	y
Ithaca	Finger Lakes	Waterfalls, Cornell Botanic Gardens	1 day
Old Forge	Adirondacks	Enchanted Forest Water	Half-day to full day

		Safari	

This region of upstate New York is where elevated wilderness meets graceful civilization, providing RVers with endless opportunities to explore at their own pace—whether it's summiting granite peaks, sipping wine beside a glacial lake, or wandering through timeless small towns with a pace as gentle as the breeze off the water.

Coastal Maine Route

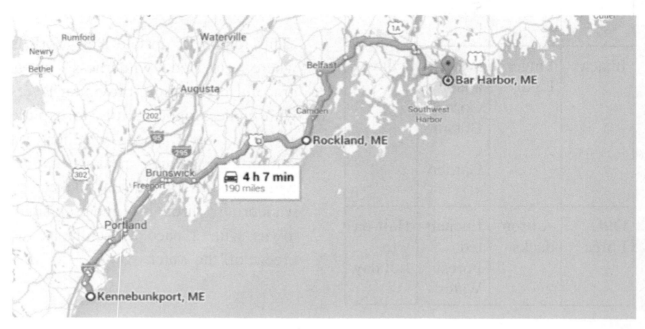

SCAN THE QR CODE

Route Overview

Start in Kittery, ME.
End: Lubec, Maine

Distance: around 300 miles (US Route 1, including picturesque spurs).

Ideal trip duration: 5-10 days Best time to visit: Late May to October.

Route Type: One-way (optional loop return inland)

Road Conditions: Most highways and byways are paved and well-maintained, with some tiny village roads and some fog-prone areas.

Route Summary

The Coastal Maine Route is a meandering, salt-kissed route that follows the Atlantic coast of New England's northeasternmost state. It runs from the southern entrance town of Kittery to the fog-draped fishing hamlet of Lubec, the easternmost point in the contiguous United States. This route follows granite-lined coats, meanders past ancient seaports, and descends into pine-scented peninsulas, each offering the marine enchantment that distinguishes Down East Maine.

Route Highlights

1. Kittery-Kennebunkport (20 miles)
Must-sees include the Kittery Trading Post, Fort McClary, the Nubble Light in York, and Kennebunkport's Dock Square.

Road Notes: US-1 northbound with minimal urban traffic and decent signage.

RV Tip: Park outside of center Kennebunkport and use shuttles or bike into town; many coastal roads here are small and congested during the summer.

2. Kennebunkport to Portland (30 Miles)
Must-see attractions include Goose Rocks Beach, Cape Elizabeth's Two Lights State Park, and Portland's Old Port.

Bite Into Maine food truck in Cape Elizabeth serves what is possibly the best lobster roll in the state.

Campgrounds include Bayley's Camping Resort (Scarborough) and Wolfe's Neck Oceanfront Camping (Freeport).

Fuel and service: Biddeford and Scarborough provide full RV services.

3. Portland-Boothbay Harbor (60 miles)
Must-sees include Freeport's iconic L.L. Bean store (open 24/7), Pemaquid Point Lighthouse, and Boothbay's Coastal Maine Botanical Gardens.

Scenic Spur: Take Route 27 south to Southport Island, which is less trafficked yet quite attractive.

Navigation Tips: Coastal fingers need slow, careful diversions; anticipate journeys to take longer than straight-line distance indicates.

4. Boothbay Harbor to Rockland/Camden (50 km).
Must-see attractions include Owls Head Lighthouse, Maine Lighthouse Museum, and Farnsworth Art Museum (Wyeth collection).

Camden Hills State Park: Outstanding views across Penobscot Bay, including hike-accessible lookouts and RV-friendly campgrounds.

Festival Watch: The Rockland Lobster Festival (August) attracts large people; make reservations well in advance.

5. Camden to Bar Harbor/Acadia National Park (80 miles).

Must-see attractions include the Penobscot Narrows Bridge Observatory, Fort Knox (Prospect), and the whole Acadia Park Loop Road.

Scenic Detour: Blue Hill Peninsula via Route 172—artistic, peaceful, and ideal for leisurely breaks.

Acadia RV Notes: The Blackwoods and Seawall campsites can accept RVs, although they book out months in advance. Some places have strict RV length limits; check beforehand.

6. Bar Harbor to Lubec (60 miles)

Must-sees include the Schoodic Peninsula (the uncrowded side of Acadia), Cutler Coast Public Lands, and the West Quoddy Head Lighthouse.

Hidden Gem: Campobello Island (via Lubec)—FDR's vacation house with stunning landscape; carry passport for Canada border crossing.

Remote Warning: Services thin out beyond Ellsworth; keep tanks full and food supplied.

Navigation and Wayfinding

The main artery is U.S. Route 1, but the charm is in the detours—state highways like ME-9, ME-15, and ME-186 lead to coastal communities and pristine shorelines.

GPS Advisory: Coastal signals may degrade; bring a paper atlas or an offline map. Many roads lack regular signage, particularly on peninsulas and parks.

Toll Alerts: Minor tolls on I-95 and various bridges (E-ZPass allowed).

Budget Breakdown (7-Day Trip Example, Two Adults)

Category	Budget RV	Mid-Range	Splurge Trip

	Trip	Trip	
Campgrounds	$175	$350	$700
Fuel (300 miles avg)	$150	$150	$150
Groceries	$150	$250	$400
Dining Out	$100	$250	$600
Attractions/Fees	$50	$100	$200
Total Estimate	**$625**	**$1,100**	**$2,050**

RV Travel Tips:

Fog and Moisture: Expect significant morning fog around coastal Maine, particularly in June and September. Drive with the lights on, limit your speed, and use dehumidifiers inside your vehicle.

Wildlife Warning: Moose and deer are common road dangers, especially at dawn and dark in the northern portions.

East of Ellsworth, there are few dump stations; prepare ahead of time and use RV park services and rest spots instead. Acadia has inadequate amenities.

Propane access is available in bigger towns (Portland, Rockland, and Ellsworth); check refill stations before venturing into more distant areas.

Insider Strategies.

Avoid Weekend Congestion: The southern coast (particularly Ogunquit, Kennebunkport, and Portland) is congested on weekends; therefore, plan to visit these regions during the week.

Lobster Pound Protocol: Most allow BYOB and offer steaming lobster on picnic tables. Payment in cash is preferable. Arrive early to ensure the freshest catch.

Photography Windows: The golden hours over the Atlantic have been flipped, with sunrises rather than sunsets taking center stage. Coastal mornings can provide spectacular illumination via mist.

The Final Mile: Why Coastal Maine?

Maine's shoreline is not a straight line; it is a braided, jagged tapestry that encourages slow driving and diversions. This path is not about speed. It's all about texture: the crunch of gravel underfoot at a lighthouse hike, the squeak of lobster boats at daybreak, and the silence of fog amid spruce woods. This voyage captures the rugged essence of the East Coast for RV travelers who choose character above convenience.

The next route is the White Mountains to Lake Champlain Corridor, which offers inland splendor as the scenery varies from sea to peak.

Southeast:

Great Smoky Mountains Explorer

Overview

The Great Smoky Mountains, which span Tennessee and North Carolina, are a complex tapestry of misty peaks, ancient woods, and Southern Appalachian history. This renowned location, known for its biodiversity, gorgeous roads, and accessible nature, is ideal for RVers looking for both tranquility and excitement.

Whether traveling along ancient byways or retiring into woodland campsites under starry nights, the Smokies provide a doorway to a timeless setting sculpted by nature and protected by heritage. With over 800 miles of hiking trails, stunning waterfalls, surviving pioneer communities, and a drive-through animal refuge, this location provides more than simply breathtaking scenery; it also provides an immersive journey into the spirit of the Southern Appalachians.

Essential RV Routes

1. Newfound Gap Road (US-441), 31 miles.

Connects: Gatlinburg, Tennessee to Cherokee, North Carolina

Highlights: Clingman's Dome spur, Newfound Gap viewpoint, and Rockefeller Memorial.

RV Notes: Paved and accessible for rigs up to 35 feet; several steep slopes and tight twists near the Dome access road; check your brakes before descending.

This primary artery through the park provides postcard vistas of spruce-fir trees and connects numerous important trailheads. The route rises approximately 5,000 feet, with several pullouts perfect for beautiful breaks.

2. Foothills Parkway (East/West)
Distance varies (33 miles finished as of 2025).

Connects: Chilhowee Lake to Sevier County, Tennessee

Highlights: Look Rock observation tower, sweeping views, low traffic

RV Notes: Class A and tow-behind vehicles may be accommodated by wide shoulders and several overlooks.

This route, designed to frame the magnificence of the Smokies, is popular among people who want to escape the crowds in Gatlinburg and Pigeon Forge. Ideal for slow drives, with plenty of opportunities to capture layered ridgelines.

3. Cades Cove circle Road - 11-mile one-way circle.

Highlights include settler cottages, deer, black bears, and John Oliver Cabin.

RV Restrictions: No RVs longer than 30 feet are permitted, and early arrival is required due to traffic congestion during peak hours.

This green valley provides the park's most accessible animal viewing. Bicycles and foot traffic predominate on designated days; check current vehicle access restrictions before entering.

Top Campgrounds for RVers
Elkmont Campground (TN) has 220 total sites, including 50+ RV-accessible ones.

Amenities include a dump station, potable water, and bathrooms (without connections).

Booking: recreation.gov; high demand. May-October

Tip: The synchronized firefly festival in June attracts large numbers; reserve six months in advance.

Nestled near the Little River, Elkmont mixes historic elegance with a tranquil environment. Trails to waterfalls and tranquil woodland treks start right from the property.

Smokemont Campground (NC) has 142 total sites and can accommodate rigs up to 40 feet.

Amenities include a dump station and flush toilets, but no electrical or water connections

Nearby: Oconaluftee Visitor Center, Mountain Farm Museum.

Smokemont is a fantastic base for visiting the park's less-trafficked North Carolina side, making it suitable for RVers looking for a less marketed environment.

Private RV parks in Pigeon Forge and Gatlinburg, TN provide luxury sites with full hookups, cable TV, and laundry facilities.

Cherokee, NC has family-friendly parks with river access and casino shuttles.

Recommended: Riveredge RV Park (Sevierville, TN) and Yogi in the Smokies (Cherokee, NC).

Local Highlights and Hidden Detours.
Roaring Fork Motor Nature Trail (Gatlinburg, TN)
Type: Narrow 6-mile circle road.

Restrictions: No trailers or RVs—use a tow vehicle or toad.

Features include cascading streams, log cabins, and trailheads to Grotto Falls and Rainbow Falls.

This close journey provides a sensory immersion into the Appalachian woods. Drives in the early morning or after a rain reveal dramatic lighting and mist clinging to moss-covered boulders.

Clingmans Dome has an elevation of 6,643 feet, making it the highest point in the park.

Access: 7-mile offshoot from Newfound Gap Road.

RV Tip: Limited RV parking; come early; no overnight parking permitted.

A paved half-mile walk leads to an observation tower with 360° views that span seven states. The temperature here might be 10-20 degrees lower than in the lowlands, so pack layers.

Cataloochee Valley

Access: gravel roads (poor clearance is not recommended for big RVs).

Wildlife: Elk herds, old structures, and peacefulness.

Tip: Consider parking your RV in Maggie Valley and daytripping with a towed vehicle

Often ignored owing to its distant approach, this historic town gives the uncommon opportunity to view bugling elk in the wild—especially stunning in fall.

Seasonal Travel Guide

Spring (March–May): Wildflower season—trilliums, dogwoods, and flaming azaleas; periodic floods in low regions.

Summer (June–August): Peak attendance, particularly in July; black bear activity rises.

Fall (September-November): Foliage spectacle attracts high traffic; weekdays are preferable for driving circles.

Winter (Dec–Feb): Many roads blocked for snow; quietest period for photography and snowshoeing

Navigation & Safety Tips

No Cell Service in Most Areas: Download downloadable maps or carry printed copies from the park visitor centers

Weather Fluctuations: Conditions may change fast at higher elevations—check forecast before treks or drives

Vehicle Restrictions: No petrol stations in the park; fill up in adjacent cities.

Altitude Braking: Use lower gears on downhill slopes; overheated brakes is a regular concern during the Newfound Gap descent.

Gatlinburg, TN is a popular tourist destination with amenities such as RV servicing, propane filling stations, food stores, and entertainment options.

Cherokee, North Carolina: Quieter, with cultural attractions including the Cherokee Indian Museum and a gateway to the Blue Ridge Parkway.

Bryson City, NC is ideal for RVers looking for outdoor outfitters, train trips, and access to the Deep Creek waterfall trails.

Suggested 3-day RV itinerary

Day 1:

Enter via Gatlinburg.

Drive Newfound Gap Road.

Hike Clingmans Dome.

Camp at Elkmont

Day 2:

Early drive to Cades Cove.

Explore pioneering structures.

Afternoon trek to Abrams Falls.

Overnight in Townsend or return to Elkmont.

Day 3:

Drive Foothills Parkway.

Detour to Look Rock.

Cross to the Cherokee side.

Visit the Oconaluftee Visitor Center and Smokemont Campground.

RV Travel Snapshot

Category	Details
Best RV Length	Under 35 ft (for park road flexibility)
Hookups in Park	None (dry camping only)
Closest Fuel Stops	Gatlinburg, Cherokee, Townsend
Dump Stations	Available at

	Smokemont and Elkmont
Recommended Season	Late Spring or Early Fall

Final Word:

The Great Smoky Mountains are more than simply a national park; they are a dynamic landscape of cultural heritage and natural beauty. This region offers more than just miles to RVers; it also provides meaning. Plan your route, prepare for mountainous terrain, and enjoy a slower pace. Within the mist and maple, the route shows more than just landscape. It conveys a feeling of location.

Florida Keys RV Escape

SCAN THE QR CODE

The Florida Keys, which stretch over 100 miles from the southern point of mainland Florida into the azure expanse of the Atlantic Ocean and Gulf of Mexico, provide an unforgettable RV trip packed with coastal beauty, abundant marine life, and sun-soaked solitude. The Overseas Highway (U.S. Route 1) is the lifeblood linking these dispersed islands, with stunning bridges and vast ocean panoramas that provide a driving experience unlike any other in the United States.

Route Overview

Begin your Florida Keys adventure at Key Largo, only an hour south of Miami, where the mainland meets island life. From here, take US 1 south past Islamorada, Marathon, and eventually Key West, the southernmost point in the continental United States. Each island town has its own set of sights and natural beauty, so making numerous pauses is crucial for soaking up the mood and recharging.

Scenic Highlights

The route is well-known for its stunning panoramic vistas, particularly from historic constructions such as the Seven Mile Bridge, where the limitless ocean appears on both sides of the road. Early morning or late afternoon drives highlight the vivid hues of sunrises and sunsets over the river, providing ideal opportunities for picture stops or peaceful contemplation at one of the many roadside pull-offs.

Essential RV Campgrounds

John Pennekamp Coral Reef State Park (Key Largo): As the first underwater park in the United States, this campsite provides full hookups and access to snorkeling, diving, and glass-bottom boat excursions of the live coral reefs. Spacious, shaded sites are ideal for bigger rigs, and

facilities include a marina, picnic spots, and a tourist center.

Founders Park Campground (Islamorada): This family-friendly facility offers beach access, sports courts, and a swimming pool. This location is suitable for individuals looking for luxury and convenience on an island.

Curry Hammock State Park (near Marathon): This campsite, known for kayaking, bird viewing, and unspoiled natural environments, offers rustic and full-hookup sites along mangrove-lined coastlines.

Boyd's Key West Campground (Key West): Located in the historic Old Town, Boyd's has several conveniences like laundry facilities, Wi-Fi, and easy access to Key West's popular nightlife and cultural activities.

Navigation Tips

Travelers should be aware that the Overseas Highway may narrow and wind rapidly on certain keys, so keeping modest speeds is critical, particularly for larger RVs. Fuel stations are few beyond Key Largo, so refilling whenever feasible is critical.

Pay heed to low clearance notices on certain bridges and causeways; although most are constructed to accept RVs, it's advisable to check your vehicle's height ahead of time.

Hidden Gems

Bahia Honda State Park: Located just off the highway near Marathon, this park has one of the Keys' most stunning beaches and good snorkeling opportunities. The ancient Bahia Honda Bridge provides amazing vistas.

Little Torch Key and Big Pine Key: These calmer islands provide animal habitats, including the opportunity to see the rare Key deer. Big Pine Key's National Key Deer Refuge provides paths and birding possibilities away from the tourist hordes.

The Turtle Hospital (Marathon) is an educational stop dedicated to the rescue and rehabilitation of sea turtles, with guided tours that raise awareness about local conservation initiatives.

Seasonal considerations

The winter months (December through April) provide great weather conditions—mild temperatures, low humidity, and little rain—drawing the most numbers. Summer and early autumn bring heat and increasing rainfall, as well as hurricane danger, so tourists should keep a careful eye on weather predictions and be ready to change their plans.

Final Notes

The Florida Keys' unique combination of natural beauty, coastal culture, and laid-back island vibes makes for an unforgettable RV experience. Planning to stop at campsites and explore on foot, bike, or kayak broadens the experience beyond the driving itself. Whether diving into the pristine seas to find bright corals or relishing delicious seafood on a waterfront pier, this vacation will provide amazing experiences for any RV traveler seeking both action and calm along America's sun-drenched southernmost route.

Bluegrass & Bourbon Trail

SCAN THE QR CODE

Kentucky's Heartbeat on Wheels: Scenic roads, timeless flavors, and historic charm.

The Bluegrass & Bourbon Trail is a must-see journey through the rolling hills and historic landscapes of central Kentucky, where America's equestrian past and bourbon heritage intersect. This road takes RV travelers through pastoral fields, ancient villages, and world-renowned distilleries, providing a mix of natural beauty, cultural depth, and exciting activities.

Route Overview

The path is centered in Lexington and runs through Fayette, Bourbon, Scott, and adjacent counties. It covers around 150 miles, although the route may be customized with diversions to accommodate diverse schedules and interests.

Start in Lexington, Kentucky.

Key stops include Keeneland Race Course, Buffalo Trace Distillery, Woodford Reserve, Four Roses, and Maker's Mark.

End: Bardstown, KY (also known as the "Bourbon Capital of the World").

Navigating the Trail

Road types include picturesque two-lane freeways, gently curving country roads, and well-maintained state routes.

Driving Conditions: The roads are generally smooth and acceptable for all RV classes, however some minor roads near distilleries and farms may be narrow or have restricted parking. Advance preparation is required for overnight breaks and day trips.

Recommended RV stops:

Lexington KOA is ideal for city access and experiencing downtown Lexington's facilities.

Bardstown Campground: Offers full hookups and is close to historic Bardstown.

Local state parks, such as Yatesville Lake State Park, provide a natural escape from the hustle and bustle of town.

Key Highlights on the Trail

1. Lexington—The Horse Capital

Lexington, the trail's entryway, is known for its verdant horse pastures and the world-renowned Keeneland Race Course. Visitors may drive over fences lined with Thoroughbred champions and visit equestrian museums. The soil in the surrounding Bluegrass area is rich in limestone, which contributes to the region's distinct bourbon taste.

2. Distillery Distinctiveness

Kentucky bourbon distilleries employ centuries-old copper pot stills and barrel warehouses, with some available for tours and tastings. Each provides a distinct perspective of bourbon-making traditions.

Buffalo Trace: One of the oldest continuously functioning distilleries, noted for its diverse bourbon offerings and profound historical origins.

Woodford Reserve: Set among horse farms, it exemplifies a painstaking, artisanal manufacturing method.

Four Roses: Known for its smooth, fruity bourbons made with a unique yeast strain and a variety of formulas.

Maker's Mark is well-known for its signature red wax-dipped bottles, which are housed in a gorgeous setting with handcrafted appeal.

3. Bardstown—Bourbon's Capital

Bardstown is the quintessential small town, with cobblestone streets, historic architecture, and a strong bourbon culture. Its attractions include the Bourbon Heritage Center and several distilleries, including Willett and Heaven Hill. The town also has local eateries serving traditional Kentucky fare, which is ideal for refueling.

Scenic Detours and Hidden Gem

Pleasant Hill Shaker Village is a preserved 19th-century Shaker community that provides a quiet cultural stop with hiking trails and historic tours.

Jacobson Park (Lexington): A peaceful lakefront area with camping and walking trails, ideal for relaxing before continuing your journey.

Napa of the Bluegrass: Head off-route to smaller, boutique distilleries tucked away on backroads that provide intimate tours and tastings without the crowds.

Tips for RV Travelers

Timing: The route is best enjoyed in the spring and autumn, when the temperature is pleasant and the scenery is vibrant. Summers may be hot and humid, while winters may bring ice on country roads.

Reservations: Popular distillery excursions often need advanced booking, particularly on weekends and holidays.

Driving Safety: Distilleries are often dispersed; consider exchanging driving duties or appointing a non-drinking driver. Local laws severely enforce DUI rules.

Waste and Water: Many distilleries lack RV facilities; schedule stops at campsites or public parks with connections to be comfortable.

Local Events: Plan your trips around events like the Kentucky Bourbon Festival (September), which provide unique experiences and bigger groups.

Sample Itinerary for 3 Days on the Bluegrass & Bourbon Trail

Day 1: Lexington & Surroundings

Morning: Tour Keeneland Race Course and see the Kentucky Horse Park.

Afternoon: Explore Buffalo Trace Distillery.

Evening: Dine in downtown Lexington and stay at a nearby RV park.

Day 2: Bourbon County Loop

Morning: Visit Woodford Reserve and Four Roses.

Afternoon: Shaker Village of Pleasant Hill diversion for history and hiking.

Evening: Stay around Versailles or Georgetown for tranquil relaxation.

Day 3: Bardstown and Beyond.

Morning tour of Maker's Mark en route to Bardstown.

Afternoon: Tour Bardstown's Bourbon Heritage Center and Willett Distillery.

Evening: Dine locally and camp overnight at the Bardstown Campground.

The Bluegrass & Bourbon Trail is a typical American tour that combines rich history with contemporary relaxation. Whether sipping small-batch bourbons or watching thoroughbreds gallop over green fields, RV travelers will find this road to be an outstanding blend of culture, nature, and workmanship.

Midwest:

Lake Michigan Circle Tour

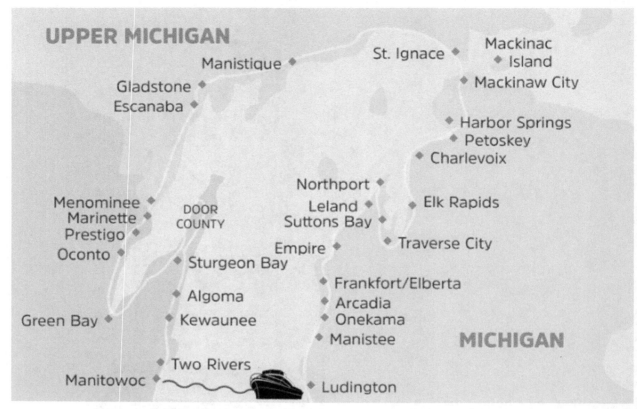

The Lake Michigan Circle Tour is an unforgettable journey around one of America's Great Lakes, combining picturesque shoreline views, vibrant cities, quaint small towns, and abundant natural parks. This journey spans over 1,300 miles and passes through four states: Illinois, Indiana, Michigan, and Wisconsin, each with its own unique environment and cultural experiences.

Overview and Route Description.

The Circle Tour follows a round around Lake Michigan, allowing RVers to begin at any point along the way. The most typical beginning point is Chicago, Illinois, which provides direct access to metropolitan facilities before continuing north along the lake's western side. The journey then bends west into Wisconsin, south into Indiana, then east into Michigan before returning to the starting point.

This circle may be done in 7 to 10 days, with flexible pauses. However, since the Lake Michigan Circle Tour offers so many possibilities for outdoor recreation, historic sites, and culinary exploration, many visitors prolong their vacation to include side excursions and leisure activities.

Key segments and highlights.

Illinois Shoreline: Chicago to Wisconsin Border.

Chicago is the biggest city on the route and serves as a vibrant gateway. RVers may visit the Navy Pier, Millennium Park, and the picturesque Lakefront Trail before continuing north. RV sites like Camp Sullivan provide easy access to local attractions and the lakefront.

Waukegan: A lesser-known port town with marinas and the Illinois Beach State Park, which has almost six miles of Lake Michigan beachfront and campsites perfect for a lovely overnight stay.

Wisconsin Coast: Racine to Door County.

Racine: Racine, known for its historic lighthouse and waterfront parks, also provides extensive architectural excursions, including Frank Lloyd Wright's early works.

Milwaukee: Wisconsin's biggest city combines metropolitan culture with waterfront beauty. RVers may visit the Milwaukee Art Museum, which has a distinctive winged design, local breweries, and wide lakefront parks. Several campsites nearby provide full hookups and easy city access.

Kohler-Andrae State Park: This park offers a peaceful refuge with almost two miles of sandy beach, wooded paths, and well-kept camping sites that can accommodate all RV sizes.

Door County is well-known for its lovely tiny villages, cherry orchards, and state parks such as Peninsula State Park, which has stunning cliffs overlooking the lake, hiking paths, and comfortable campsites.

Indiana Shore: Michigan City to Burns Harbor.

Indiana Dunes National Park: The dunes, which stretch 15 miles along Lake Michigan's coastline, contain distinct habitats and numerous hiking routes. Campgrounds inside the park provide RVers the necessary facilities and are close to the beach.

Michigan City: Known for its lighthouse and outlet shopping, the city has multiple RV sites and is a handy stop before entering Michigan.

Michigan Shore: St. Joseph to Traverse City St. Joseph is a traditional lakefront town with historic lighthouses, beaches, and a charming downtown with boutique shops and restaurants. RV parks are abundant and provide good lake access.

Grand Haven's lakeside campgrounds, known for their musical fountains and sandy beaches, are perfect for extended stays.

Muskegon: Featuring Lake Michigan's largest state park, Muskegon State Park, which includes campgrounds, dunes, and swimming areas.

Ludington: A lively harbor town with a state park that provides camping, hiking, and beach access.

Traverse City, the northern anchor of the Lake Michigan Circle Tour, combines urban sophistication with outdoor adventure, including vineyards, cherry farms, and the nearby Sleeping Bear Dunes National Lakeshore. Traverse City is well-equipped with numerous full-service RV parks.

Scenic Byways & Routes to Prioritize

US Highway 12 (Illinois and Wisconsin) runs parallel to much of the lakefront, providing scenic lakeside drives and easy access to both urban and natural sites.

Highways 42 and 57 (Wisconsin Door Peninsula): Winding roads with panoramic lake views, small-town charm, and numerous state parks.

M-22 (Michigan): Perhaps the most recognizable stretch, this route skirts the northwest shore of Michigan's Lower Peninsula. It provides spectacular vistas, historic lighthouses, and access to Sleeping Bear Dunes. The road is a must-drive for RVers looking for scenic views and attractive towns like Leland and Glen Arbor.

RV Travel Tips for the Lake Michigan Circle Tour.

Timing: The greatest weather and full availability of campsites and attractions occur in late spring and early autumn (May to October).

Reservations are suggested during peak summer months, since demand might be high.

Campground Selection: The Circle Tour provides a combination of state parks, private RV resorts, and municipal campgrounds. Expect a variety of facilities, with some sites offering full connections and others more primitive. Plan appropriately depending on your RV's specifications.

Fuel and amenities: While major cities along the road provide plenty of refueling and service choices, smaller areas, particularly on the Door Peninsula or in northern Michigan, may have limited amenities. Stock up before going into less crowded regions.

Navigation: In isolated places, cellular connectivity may be patchy, so bring current paper maps or offline GPS navigation. The official Lake Michigan Circle Tour signage helps with route finding, but always checks with maps to prevent diversions.

Weather Considerations: Lake Michigan's weather may change quickly, especially in the spring and autumn. High winds and fog are typical around the shorelines; use care while driving and camping near dunes or cliffs.

Activities: Schedule time for hiking, biking, and water sports. Most state parks and natural regions provide rental equipment or guided excursions, making it simple to immerse in the environment without heavy gear.

Hidden Gems & Local Favorites
Frank Lloyd Wright's Wingspread (Racine, WI): A stunning example of Prairie School architecture that is accessible for public visits.

Fishtown, Leland, MI: A historic fishing community with maintained shanties, galleries, and artisan stores.

Indiana Dunes Taltree Arboretum: A lesser-known botanical park tucked among the dunes, suitable for nature treks.

Sheboygan, WI: Known as the "Bratwurst Capital of the World," it also boasts picturesque lakeside walks and well-kept campsites.

Tunnel Park, St. Joseph, MI: Features a man-made tunnel leading to a sandy beach with spectacular cliffs.

Summary

The Lake Michigan Circle Tour is an excellent RV route for those looking for a mix of urban sophistication, natural beauty, and historic charm along one of North America's most picturesque lakeshores. With careful preparation, this loop can provide a dynamic, holistic road trip experience, emphasizing historic cities, peaceful seaside towns, and breathtaking natural vistas. The Lake Michigan Circle Tour is a timeless trip filled with exploration, comfort, and unending visual beauty for RV enthusiasts looking to experience the Great Lakes at their best.

Badlands & Black Hills Trek

South Dakota's rugged heartland provides a riveting combination of unearthly vistas, historic sites, and lively culture, making the Badlands and Black Hills adventure a must-see for every RV traveler. This itinerary strikes a balance between breathtaking natural scenery, immersive history, and must-see attractions, all of which are easily navigable with expert tips tailored to RV travelers.

Overview

The Badlands and Black Hills adventure spans roughly 350 miles from east to west and includes magnificent geological formations, historic monuments, and small villages steeped in Western tradition. The trip starts in the harsh, steeply eroded Badlands National Park and continues westward into the wooded, granite-dotted Black Hills, which are home to Mount Rushmore and Custer State Park.

The ideal travel season runs from late spring to early fall, when weather conditions favor both road safety and outdoor exploration. Winter travel needs care owing to icy roads and minimal amenities, particularly in the park's remote areas.

Key destinations and scenic routes

1. Badlands National Park.

Entry Point: Interior, SD (via SD Highway 240).

Highlights include jagged spires, deep valleys, and broad plains. The Badlands Loop Road (Highway 240) is a 31-mile paved highway with several pullouts for photography and short treks such as the Notch Trail and Fossil Exhibit Trail.

RV Considerations: Several campsites accommodate RVs, including the Cedar Pass Campground, which has full hookups and easy access. Larger rigs benefit from wider roads and better signage.

2. Wall Drug Town and Visitor Center.

Location: Wall, SD, right beyond the Badlands' eastern border.

Features: This historic station is known for its kitschy appeal, free ice water, and substantial shopping. Ideal for replenishment and a respite between lengthy travels.

RV Tips: Designated parking fits big RVs; high season may need patience.

3. Rapid City Gateway.

Approach: Exit Badlands and go west on I-90 to Rapid City

Significance: Rapid City, known as the "Gateway to the Black Hills," has a wide range of amenities, including RV campgrounds, repair shops, and groceries.

Navigation: Use Rapid City as a base or staging point before entering more remote Black Hills terrain.

4. Mount Rushmore National Memorial

Access: SD Highway 244 off I-90 near Keystone

Features: Iconic presidential statues cut into granite cliffs. The facility features a museum, walking paths, and informative events.

RV Notes: The parking area can accommodate big RVs; early arrival is encouraged during the summer months to minimize congestion.

5) Custer State Park

Location: South of Rapid City, accessible via US Highway 16A (Iron Mountain Road).

Experience: Wildlife watching (bison herds, pronghorns), picturesque roads with severe switchbacks, and historical places. The Needles Highway, with its granite spires and tunnels, is a must-drive road, however vehicle length is limited (35 feet maximum).

Camping: Multiple campsites with complete RV facilities; prior reservations are recommended during the busy season.

6) Deadwood

Historic Town: Recognized for its Wild West heritage, casinos, and thriving downtown.

RV Parking: Designated locations near town, with fuel and grocery stores close.

Navigation Tips for RVers

Road Restrictions: The Needles Highway and other Black Hills highways include tight bends and tunnels with severe length limitations, so check vehicle size before trying.

Fuel Stops: Fuel is widely accessible in Rapid City, Wall, and Deadwood; but, services are limited inside the park borders; refuel before venturing into isolated locations.

Weather Preparedness: Summer thunderstorms may create unexpected road closures in the Badlands; keep an eye on local circumstances and pack emergency supplies.

Cellular service is limited in Badlands National Park and several Black Hills locations. Download offline maps and GPS routes before leaving.

Waste Disposal: Public dump facilities may be located in Rapid City and at certain campsites. Plan your garbage disposal properly.

Suggested itinerary (4-5 days)

Day 1: Take SD-240 into Badlands National Park, then finish the Badlands Loop Road and walk one or two short trails before spending the night at Cedar Pass Campground.

Day 2: Drive to Wall, SD; tour Wall Drug; drive west to Rapid City; spend the night at an RV campground in Rapid City.

Day 3: Visit Mount Rushmore in the morning; then drive along Iron

Mountain Road into Custer State Park, where you'll camp overnight.

Day 4: Wildlife loop in Custer State Park; exploration of Sylvan Lake and hiking trails; late afternoon trip to Deadwood; overnight stay near Deadwood.

Day 5: Tour historic Deadwood; prepare for departure or extend your journey to the adjacent Black Hills sites.

Budget Breakdown (Per Day, Approximated)

Expense Category	Estimate (USD)
RV Campground Fees	$30 - $60
Fuel	$40 - $80
Food & Supplies	$20 - $50
Park Entrance Fees	$10 - $30
Miscellaneous	$10 - $25

Packing checklist for this trek includes durable hiking boots and layered clothes.

Sun protection (hat, sunscreen, and sunglasses)

Portable water containers (water sources are scarce).

Emergency roadside kit with tire repair tools

Offline maps and printed park brochures

Binoculars for wildlife viewing.

This journey captures the essence of South Dakota's rugged natural beauty and storied history, rewarding RV travelers with breathtaking views and authentic experiences. Proper preparation and adherence to park restrictions guarantee a safe and pleasurable visit across this breathtaking landscape.

Ozarks Scenic Drive

SCAN THE QR CODE

America's most lovely and varied environments. Stretching throughout southern Missouri and northern Arkansas, this road is a treasure trove of craggy hills, green woods, dazzling lakes, and attractive tiny towns. For RV travelers, the Ozarks offer a combination of accessible highways, breathtaking views, and numerous recreational possibilities, making it an important component to any road trip plan.

Route Overview

The Ozarks Scenic Drive provides an unforgettable tour through one of

The trip largely follows a circle covering elements of Missouri's Route 76 and Arkansas's Highway 7, snaking into the heart of the Ozark Mountains. The overall trip spans around 200 miles, making it suitable for a 2-3 day tour, with several pauses to explore nature, local culture, and outdoor activities.

Start Point: Branson, Missouri

End Point: Hot Springs, Arkansas

Length: around 200 miles.

The best time to visit is late spring to early autumn (May-October) for lush vegetation and good road conditions; fall for magnificent foliage.

Highlights and Key Stops

1. Branson, Missouri.

Branson, a thriving entertainment town, serves as the entrance to the Ozarks Scenic Drive. Beyond theaters and family activities, it has well-equipped RV parks and service facilities to help you prepare for the road ahead.

2. Table Rock Lake and Dam.

The course hugs Table Rock Lake, a large reservoir famed for its crystal-clear waters and good fishing,

boating, and swimming opportunities. The dam region features magnificent viewpoints excellent for a little pause and photo opportunity.

3. Silver Dollar City.

This 1880s-themed amusement park nestled in the hills is worth a visit for families traveling together. It combines entertainment with the natural splendor of the Ozarks, surrounded by wooded cliffs.

4. The Buffalo National River, Arkansas.

Crossing into Arkansas, the route follows the Buffalo National River, one of the few free-flowing rivers in the United States. Numerous access spots provide options for canoeing, hiking, and animal viewing. The river's limestone bluffs, caves, and waterfalls are notable features.

5) Mount Magazine State Park

Mount Magazine, at 2,753 feet, is Arkansas' highest mountain. The park offers panoramic views, hiking paths, and rocky terrain ideal for RVers looking for a wilderness vacation. During the summer, the summit's milder environment provides a welcome relief.

6) Hot Springs, Arkansas

The trip ends at Hot Springs, a town known for its hot springs and medieval buildings. The oldest federal reserve, Hot Springs National Park, offers RV travelers the opportunity to soak in natural hot springs or explore hiking trails.

scenic features and road conditions

The Ozarks Scenic Drive is distinguished by winding, two-lane routes that serpentine across rolling hills and lush woodlands. Elevation changes are common yet doable in conventional RVs. The pavement condition is typically decent, however certain portions near the Buffalo River might be narrow and need careful navigation.

There are several roadside pull-offs with interpretive signs, picnic sites, and viewpoints that provide panoramic views of valleys and peaks covered in oak and hickory trees. Wildlife sightings are common—deer, wild turkeys, and even black bears—so drive cautiously.

RV Facilities and Services

Along the way, cities like Branson, Eureka Springs, and Harrison provide full-service RV parks with hookups, gas stations, and repair shops. Primitive camping is allowed in national and state parks, although popular locations fill up rapidly during high seasons. Reservations for camping near major areas such as Buffalo National River are advised well in advance.

Travel Tips for RVers

Fuel Planning: Gas stations are spaced out, especially on the Arkansas section. If you are uncertain, carry extra gasoline.

Weather Awareness: Sudden afternoon thunderstorms are common in the summer; check forecasts and plan accordingly.

Wildlife Warning: Reduce your speed at dawn and dusk to avoid animal collisions.

Local Cuisine: Roadside eateries provide area delicacies such as fried catfish and Ozark trout.

Cell coverage is scarce in rural places, so obtain offline maps and instructions before leaving.

The Ozarks Scenic Drive captures the essence of American natural beauty and small-town charm, providing an unforgettable experience for RV enthusiasts. Its mix of scenic vistas, outdoor adventure, and cultural stops creates a multifaceted route ideal for the freedom of RV travel.

Southwest:

Grand Circle National Parks

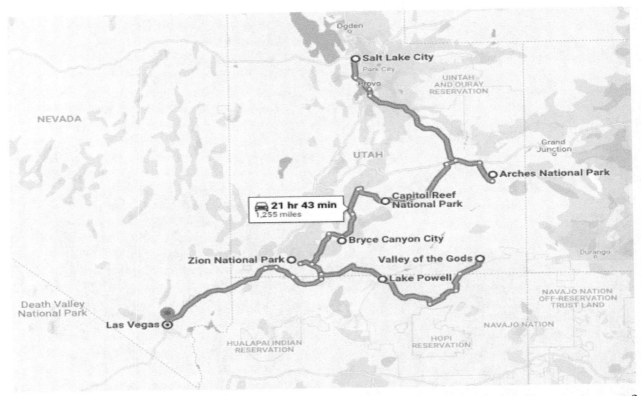

SCAN THE QR CODE

The Grand Circle is a famous area of the American Southwest that includes a collection of national parks, monuments, and spectacular landscapes covering around 200,000 square miles across Utah, Arizona, Colorado, and New Mexico. This huge stretch has some of the country's most spectacular natural marvels and provides an unequaled opportunity for RV travelers seeking dramatic desert landscapes, red rock formations, and old cultural sites.

Key Parks Within the Grand Circle.

Zion National Park, Utah

Zion's high sandstone cliffs and tiny slot canyons make it a popular destination for RVers. The park's Zion Canyon Scenic Drive is a must-see, but be aware that private car access is limited during high seasons due to the shuttle system. RVers should use authorized campsites, such as Watchman or South Campground, which are both designed for bigger rigs. From Zion, visit the lesser-known Kolob Canyons for quiet and breathtaking views.

Bryce Canyon National Park, Utah

Bryce Canyon, known for its unearthly hoodoos (tall, thin spires of rock), provides panoramic views that shift greatly with the light. The major loop route is accessible to RVs, but drivers should be mindful of tight curves and steep hills. Ruby's Inn Campground, located outside the park, has full hookups and facilities suitable for RV stays. Sunrise and Sunset Point are readily accessible vistas ideal for RV day trips.

Arches National Park, Utah

This park's scenery is more dry and rough, with approximately 2,000 natural stone arches. RV guests will find the park's paved roads accessible, but they should be warned that campsite amenities are minimal. The neighboring Devil's Garden campsite is the only established campsite in the park, with no connections but plenty of room for bigger RVs. Off-peak trips offer for a more relaxed study of prominent arches such as Delicate Arch and Landscape Arch.

Canyonlands National Park (Utah

Canyonlands is divided into four districts: Island in the Sky, The Needles, The Maze, and the Rivers. Its landscape ranges from spectacular mesa tops to lonely wilderness. The Island in the Sky region is primarily accessible by RV, with paved roads and picturesque vistas. Backcountry RV travelers must prepare ahead of time owing to difficult, gravel routes in other regions. RV parking and camping are best available outside the park, in adjacent communities such as Moab.

Capitol Reef National Park (Utah

Capitol Reef, a lesser-known jewel, has remarkable geology, including the Waterpocket Fold, a nearly 100-mile monocline. RV-friendly roads include the paved Scenic Drive and the historic Fruita region, where the campsite has minimal facilities and room for bigger rigs. The park's peaceful atmosphere makes it an ideal stopover for RVers seeking to avoid crowds while enjoying hiking, orchards, and historic buildings.

Monument Valley Navajo Tribal Park (Arizona / Utah border)

Monument Valley is an important part of the Grand Circle experience, despite not being a national park. The renowned red sandstone buttes are best explored on Navajo-guided tours, but the surrounding road is accessible to RVs with modest clearance. There are no built campsites within the park, but adjacent RV parks in Kayenta, AZ, provide complete amenities and convenient access.

Grand Canyon National Park (Ariz.)

While just beyond the inner Grand Circle, the Grand Canyon's North Rim embodies the region's ethos. The North Rim provides a calmer, more secluded RV experience than the South Rim, which is regularly frequented. The North Rim Campground can accommodate RVs but does not provide connections.

Reservations are advised well in advance. The South Rim includes many RV-accessible campsites, although they tend to be congested, necessitating advance preparation.

RVers' Must-Know Navigation and Travel Tips

Road Conditions and Access: Most Grand Circle sites are accessible by paved roads designed for big RVs. However, some interior park roads, particularly scenic or backcountry routes, may have size or clearance limits. Always check park websites for the most recent road conditions and vehicle restrictions.

Campground Reservations: Due to the popularity of Grand Circle parks, campgrounds fill up rapidly, particularly in the spring, summer, and autumn. Early bookings, usually six months to a year in advance, are highly recommended. If the park campsites are full, consider overflow camping in adjacent towns.

Fuel and Supplies: Gas stations and RV repair centers may not be available on remote sections between sites. Before approaching more remote places, stock up on gasoline, water, and food, particularly if you're taking a long route via Canyonlands or the Capitol Reef.

Seasonal Considerations: Summers may be very hot, with temperatures surpassing 100°F, while winters can bring snow and road closures, especially in higher elevation parks such as Bryce Canyon and the Grand Canyon's North Rim. Spring and autumn provide the most pleasant weather and least congested settings.

Navigation Technology: GPS systems may suffer in deep gorges or isolated locations. Carry physical maps and utilize applications that allow for offline navigation. Cell service may be restricted or nonexistent in certain areas of the Grand Circle.

Vehicle Preparedness: Check your RV's brakes, tires, and cooling system. Steep gradients and steep descents are commonplace. Drivers should be familiar with mountain and desert driving situations, such as tight, curving roads.

Suggested RV Routes & Itineraries

The Classic Grand Circle Loop (about. 1,000 miles) begins and ends in Las Vegas, covering Zion, Bryce Canyon, Capitol Reef, Arches, Canyonlands, Monument Valley, and the North Rim of the Grand Canyon. This tour combines renowned monuments, beautiful drives, and cultural events within reasonable daily travel distances.

The Southern Highlights Route focuses on Monument Valley and the Grand Canyon, making it perfect for RVers who want to spend more time studying Navajo culture and the breathtaking scenery.

Explore Utah's "Mighty Five" parks (Zion, Bryce, Capitol Reef, Arches, and Canyonlands) on the Utah Explorer Route, designed for RV travelers looking to optimize their time in the various landscapes of southern Utah.

This book is meant to provide RV travelers with the information they need to plan confidently, maneuver quickly, and enjoy the Grand Circle's grandeur in comfort and safety. Each park provides unique opportunities for exploration, and when combined, they form one of America's most breathtaking road trip destinations.

Route 66 Highlights

Route 66, which runs roughly 2,448 miles from Chicago, Illinois to Santa Monica, California, is considered the archetypal American road trip. Often referred to as the "Main Street of America," this historic roadway exposes a patchwork of nostalgic monuments, lively little towns, and various landscapes that capture the essence of cross-country travel.

Illinois: The Starting Point

The voyage starts in the urban bustle of Chicago, where Route 66 takes form on city streets dotted with old eateries and neon lights. As the highway goes southwest, cities like Joliet and Pontiac have traditional roadside attractions such as Mother Road museums, rebuilt gas stations, and tacky hotels from the mid-twentieth century. The combination of early automotive heritage and Midwestern charm sets the tone for the journey ahead.

Missouri: Gateway to the West.

Route 66 crosses the Mississippi River and traverses through Missouri's heartland, with St. Louis serving as a major metropolitan destination. The magnificent Gateway Arch frames this portion, while the city's historic districts provide views into the highway's impact on cultural growth. Further west, villages like Cuba and Springfield are adorned with old paintings and roadside eateries selling substantial meals. The route across Missouri is famous for its preservation efforts, with many historic roadbeds and neon signs still intact.

Kansas: The shortest passage.

SCAN THE QR CODE

<u>**Kansas**</u>

Kansas has just 13 miles of Route 66, yet it has plenty of flavor. The little hamlet of Galena celebrates classic Americana with restored autos and old paintings honoring the highway's history. The serene rural terrain provides a pleasant contrast to busy states, making it ideal for RVers looking for a quick yet memorable trip.

Oklahoma: Cultural Crossroads

Oklahoma's Route 66 route is brimming with Native American heritage, wayside art, and distinctive roadside architecture. Tulsa and Oklahoma City combine sophisticated metropolitan experiences with Route 66 heritage. The Blue Whale of Catoosa, a whimsical roadside sculpture, personifies the playful spirit that pervades this stretch. Oklahoma's long stretch of Route 66 is lined with renovated hotels and long-standing restaurants, many of which are still maintained by families that remember the road's glory days.

Texas: The Panhandle Experience

Route 66 travels across the Texas Panhandle, a harsh, open region with broad sky and infinite vistas. Amarillo serves as the primary center, including the famed Cadillac Ranch art piece, which has buried and painted Cadillacs that provide an interactive experience for visitors. This part emphasizes the sharp contrasts between natural beauty and roadside culture, with eateries and old-fashioned service stations maintained as artifacts of bygone eras.

New Mexico: Enchantment on the Road.

New Mexico's Route 66 section combines Southwestern culture, ancient pueblos, and stunning desert landscapes. Albuquerque's Old Town has adobe architecture and bustling markets, while Santa Fe, just north of the route, entices with world-renowned art and gastronomy. Along the roadway, neon-lit hotels and eccentric roadside attractions provide color and character, resulting in a distinct combination of Route 66 nostalgia with Native American influence.

Arizona: Desert Majesty.

Route 66 in Arizona passes through spectacular scenery, including the Painted Desert and areas of Petrified Forest National Park. Vintage hotels and eateries may still be found in towns like Holbrook and Flagstaff, adding to the nostalgic feel of the route. The portion near the Grand Canyon is a natural highlight, with easy excursions to one of the country's most recognized sights. The Arizona segment highlights Route 66's unique blend of natural wonders and historic Americana.

California: The Pacific Finale.

The last section of Route 66 runs from the Mojave Desert via Los Angeles to the Pacific Ocean. Barstow and San Bernardino provide traditional roadside attractions, while the route's approach to Los Angeles immerses visitors in the urban sprawl that contrasts with previous rural areas. The voyage concludes at the Santa Monica Pier, a symbolic endpoint where the roadway meets the ocean. California's Route 66 section combines metropolitan culture, desert landscapes, and seaside vistas, providing a dramatic climax to the cross-country journey.

Key Tips for RV Travelers on Route 66

Road Conditions: Some sections of Route 66 have been rebuilt by modern roadways, while others remain tiny, twisting, or unpaved. Consult thorough maps and local guides to find drivable parts appropriate for bigger RVs.

Historic Sites: Many famous sites are only open during certain seasons or hours. Plan your trips ahead of time and double-check the hours of operation, particularly in small towns.

Fuel and services: Amenities in rural areas may be limited. Fill up frequently, carry extra water, and check for RV-friendly campgrounds along the way.

Cultural Sensitivity: Route 66 runs through Native American lands and communities. Respect local traditions and, if feasible, support indigenous-owned companies.

Seasonal Considerations: Summer temperatures, particularly in the southern deserts, may be harsh. Winter travel in northern states may include snow; plan appropriately.

Must-See Stop Summary

Illinois: Route 66 Hall of Fame (Pontiac); Gemini Giant (Wilmington).

Missouri: Gateway Arch (St. Louis); Route 66 Mural City (Cuba).

Kansas: Historic Galena Murals

Oklahoma: Blue Whale of Catoosa, Route 66 Museum in Clinton.

Texas: Cadillac Ranch (Amarillo)

New Mexico: Albuquerque Old Town and Santa Fe (nearby)

Arizona: Painted Desert, Petrified Forest, Grand Canyon Access.

California: Barstow Route 66 Museum and Santa Monica Pier

The Route 66 adventure is more than a drive; it is a cultural mosaic that connects decades of American history with the landscapes and people that fashioned the nation's automotive and tourism legacy. For RV explorers in 2025, it remains a captivating voyage through time, nostalgia, and discovery.

Texas Hill Country Adventure

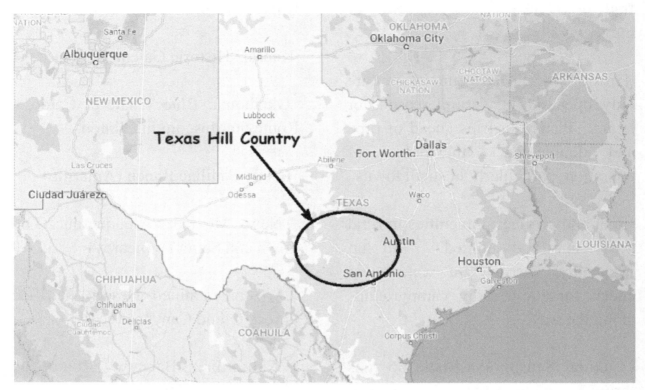

Overview:

The Texas Hill Country, located between Austin and San Antonio, is an area where limestone cliffs meet cypress-lined rivers, German historical villages provide peach cobbler and bratwurst, and spring wildflowers paint the roadside in vibrant blues and reds. This central Texas area winds through oak-dotted hills and whispering fields, providing RVers with a winning combination of rustic charm, cultural depth, and natural beauty. From ancient dance halls to river tubing, high wine tastings to ghost villages, this journey catches the heart of the Lone Star State with ease and personality.

Primary Route: Hill Country Loop (Austin to Bandera and back).

Approximately 320 miles.
Recommended duration is 5-7 days.
Best travel windows: March-May (wildflower season) and October-November (cooler temperatures, less tourists).

Core Towns and Waypoints:

From Austin, go via Dripping Springs, Johnson City, Fredericksburg, Kerrville, Bandera, Medina, Blanco, Wimberley, and back to Austin.

Route Breakdown and Key Stops

1. Austin to Dripping Springs - 25 miles.

SCAN THE QR CODE

Austin to Dripping Springs

Route: US-290W.

Terrain: Gradual elevation change, large highways with occasional tiny rural lanes.

Must-See:

Hamilton Pool Preserve has a collapsed grotto and a natural swimming hole with a fern-draped limestone overhang.

Bell Springs Winery: Perfect for a leisurely sampling among the oak trees.

Cottonwood Creek RV Park has quiet sites with full hookups tucked amid trees.

2. Dripping Springs to Johnson City is 30 miles.

SCAN THE QR CODE

Dripping Springs to Johnson City

Route: US-290W.

Scenic Features: Rolling pastures, occasional longhorn sightings, and roadside wildflower stands.

Must-See:

Pedernales Falls State Park: A popular spot for waterfall treks, bird viewing, and stargazing.

Science Mill: An interactive STEM museum ideal for families.

Historical significance: Lyndon B. Johnson's childhood home is preserved here.

3. Johnson City to Fredericksburg - 30 miles

SCAN THE QR CODE

Route: Continue on US-290W.

Cultural Crossroads: This stretch crosses into Texas German territory.

Must-See:

Main Street is packed with stores, biergartens, bakers, and museums.

The National Museum of the Pacific War is a world-class military museum located in the middle of town.

Campground Highlight: Lady Bird Johnson Municipal Park RV Park - Clean, inexpensive, and close to nature trails and golf courses.

Bonus Excursion: Visit Enchanted Rock State Natural Area for granite dome climbs and panoramic vistas.

4. Fredericksburg to Kerrville: 25 miles.

Route: TX-16S

Driving Notes: Two-lane roads that curve gently with lovely valley dips.

Must-See:

Kerrville River Trail: A flat, picturesque trail ideal for biking or a leisurely riverside walk.

The Museum of Western Art celebrates cowboy culture and frontier artwork.

SCAN THE QR CODE

Fredericksburg to Kerrville

5. Kerrville to Bandera - 25 miles

Route: TX-173 S

Wild West Legacy: Bandera proclaims itself as the "Cowboy Capital of the World."

Must-See:

11th Street Cowboy Bar: Live music beneath the stars with a genuine honky-tonk feel.

Dude Ranches: Book a day ride or an overnight stay for an authentic cowboy experience.

Skyline Ranch RV Park has peaceful, wide spaces with access to the Medina River.

6. Bandera to Medina to Blanco (60 kilometers)

Route: TX-16 N → TX-173 N → FM 2325

Scenic Features: Hilltops, high meadows, and serpentine descents.

Must-See:

Medina, the apple capital, is famous for its orchards and fresh-pressed cider.

Blanco State Park offers gentle tubing, swimming, and riverside barbecues along the Blanco River.

7. Blanco to Wimberley to Austin (80 miles)

Route: FM 165 to RR 12 N.

The last stretch is a picturesque return route via stream valleys and limestone cliffs.

Must-See:

Wimberley Blue Hole: Crystal-clear swimming in a shady creek—a local gem.

Market Days (first Saturdays) is one of the state's oldest outdoor marketplaces.

Campground Highlight: RV Park at La Hacienda (Austin) - Full facilities and views of Lake Travis.

Hidden Gems and Side Trips

Luckenbach, TX: This little hamlet, just outside Fredericksburg, has a strong musical presence. Almost every day, a live country jam takes place beneath oak trees.

Willow City Loop: A 13-mile diversion north of Fredericksburg, this small ranch road provides some of the greatest wildflower views in Texas.

Devil's Backbone Scenic Drive is a winding road that connects Wimberley with Blanco. Stop at the Devil's Backbone Overlook for panoramic views.

Practical considerations

Fuel stops: Keep an eye on the tank west of Fredericksburg and around Medina. Gas stations might be spread widely in rural areas.

RV Services:

Kerrville RV Station offers repairs, parts, and maintenance.

Texas Hill Country RV Repair - Fredericksburg offers mobile RV tech services.

Cell coverage is good in towns, but expect dead zones in state parks and along FM roads. Prepare ahead of time by downloading offline maps.

Budget Snapshot (Per Day For Two Travelers)

Category	Budget ($)	Mid-Range ($)	Premium ($)
RV Park Fees	30	50	90
Fuel	40	40	40

(avg. 10 mpg)			
Food & Dining	25	60	120
Attractions & Tours	10	30	60
Total Daily Estimate	**105**	**180**	**310**

Wildflower Alert

Peak flowering occurs from mid-March to April. Bluebonnets, Indian paintbrushes, and coreopsis bloom on the roadsides and ranchlands, particularly along US-290 and the Willow City Loop.

Navigation Tips

RV GPS is recommended for highways with low clearance bridges and steep slopes. Apps such as RV LIFE Trip Wizard and Garmin RV GPS versions are designed for big vehicles.

Turnaround Caution: Narrow hill roads (such as RR 1888) have limited turnouts. Plan routes that enable looping returns instead of backtracking.

Flash floods may occur in low-lying regions after spring rainfall. Avoid dry stream banks during the storm season.

Conclusion:

The Texas Hill Country is a masterclass in laid-back adventure, natural beauty, and small-town Americana. Its mix of convenient campsites, meandering backroads, and cultural icons make it a great place for RVers looking for more than simply destinations—here, the trip is the goal.

Route verified for 2025, with updated campground availability and road conditions.

West:

California Coast & Wine Country

Overview

SCAN THE QR CODE

The California Coast & Wine Country route is a sensory feast that runs from the foggy coastlines of the Redwood Empire to the sun-soaked vineyards of the Central Coast. This route offers a panoramic view of spectacular cliffs, coastal breezes, redwood forests, and world-renowned wine districts, all connected by Highway 1, Highway 101, and picturesque byways that wind through golden valleys and ancient villages.

Designed for RVers who want to experience both the cinematic majesty of the Pacific and the gentle joys of wine tasting and small-town discovery, this route rewards careful preparation with spectacular stops and seamless logistics.

Key Route Highlights

Region	Main Highways	Top Attractions	Best RV Parks
North Coast	US-101	Avenue of the Giants, Mendocino, Fort Bragg	Benbow KOA, Caspar Beach RV Park
Wine Country	CA-29, CA-12	Napa Valley, Sonoma, Calistoga	Napa Valley Expo RV Park, Sonoma County Fairgrounds
Bay Area	US-101, I-280	San Francisco, Golden Gate	San Francisco RV Resort, Marin
		Bridge, Half Moon Bay	RV Park
Central Coast	CA-1	Santa Cruz, Big Sur, San Simeon	Ventana Campground, Morro Dunes RV Park
Santa Ynez Valley	CA-154	Solvang, Los Olivos, Lake Cachuma	Flying Flags RV Resort, Lake Cachuma Recreation Area

Regional Guide

1. Redwood Empire to Mendocino Coast.

Begin your drive where the giants live. The northernmost portions of the coast in Eureka and Arcata have rough appeal and old-growth redwoods that tower above Highway 101. Detour to the Avenue of the Giants, a 31-mile alternative path through cathedral-like woodland. Southward, the shoreline gets more rough and personal. Mendocino and Fort Bragg have beachfront cliff hikes, Victorian architecture, and access to glass beaches and tidal pools.

RV Tip: The narrow roads on CA-1 between Leggett and Mendocino demand attention. Class A rigs longer than 30 feet may struggle with tight turns. If you're in a huge coach, try rejoining CA-1 farther south on CA-20.

2. Napa and Sonoma Wine Country.

This is California wine country in its peak. Napa Valley and Sonoma County are not only rich in wine, but they also provide RV-friendly facilities. CA-29 runs through historic communities like St. Helena and Yountville, while CA-12 provides a more tranquil experience in Sonoma. While many vineyards do not allow RVs, some provide adjacent overnight accommodations and shuttle services.

Recommended stops:

Castello di Amorosa (Napa) is a medieval-style winery with RV parking in adjacent Calistoga.

Benziger Family Winery (Sonoma): Certified biodynamic, with small rig parking.

Navigation Avoid going through downtown Napa on weekends, since congestion is usual. Use Silverado Trail as a parallel north-south route.

3. San Francisco Bay Area.

Though difficult for huge trucks, the benefits of transiting the Bay Area are significant. Plan ahead: urban congestion and bridge tolls need smart entrance and departure points. Marin County, situated north of the Golden Gate Bridge, provides excellent staging areas for trips into San Francisco. If possible, avoid driving your RV over the Golden Gate Bridge and instead park and use public transportation.

Must-Sees:

Muir Woods National Monument: Tall redwoods near the city. There is limited RV parking; please use the shuttle from Mill Valley.

Half Moon Bay: Oceanfront camping with city access. Make your reservations many months in advance.

4. Monterey to Big Sur.

This famed section of CA-1 carves between cliffs, hugging the Pacific with each turn. It's more than simply a drive; it's a cinematic experience. Expect tight roadways with no shoulders and sharp drop-offs. RVers must be precise and patient. Big Sur's splendor is only rivaled by the rarity of large-rig pullouts and camping. Book early and understand your limitations.

Top RV Friendly Stops:

Ventana Campground (Big Sur) accommodates only tents and modest RVs.

Big Sur Campground & Cabins accepts RVs up to 30 feet long.

Morro Bay State Park (south of Big Sur) is more accessible and offers views of the ocean and estuary.

Road Advisory: The CA-1 is prone to landslides and closures. Always check Caltrans before departing.

5. Santa Barbara and Wine Valleys.

The Santa Ynez Valley is located south of the Central Coast, and it combines cowboy tradition with elegant vineyards. Solvang, a Danish-themed hamlet, is a fun visit, while Los Olivos has strong wine credentials in a relaxed environment. CA-154 is a picturesque diversion off US-101, passing through undulating hills and shady valleys.

Camping Favorites:

Flying Flags RV Resort: High-end facilities with a resort vibe.

Lake Cachuma Recreation Area offers waterfront campsites, nature walks, and access to wine regions.

Local Tip: Tastings and reservations at major vineyards are more quiet on weekdays. Many tasting rooms in Solvang and Los Olivos are walkable from authorized RV parking areas.

Scenic Side Trips (Detours Worth Driving)
Point Reyes National Seashore has wildlife, lighthouses, and breathtaking seascapes. Best accessible from Petaluma or Novato.

Paso Robles Wine Country: This AVA, located east of the coast, has robust reds as well as geothermal hot springs. Use CA-46 from Cambria or Templeton.

Hearst Castle in San Simeon: Visit the opulent estate and spend the night at nearby San Simeon State Park.

Seasonal guidance

Spring brings wildflowers in Sonoma and clear skies along Big Sur. Ideal for shoulder-season travel with fewer crowds.

Summer is peak season—campgrounds fill quickly, particularly in Big Sur and Napa. Make your reservations early.

Fall is grape harvest season, and wineries are buzzing with activity. Fog decreases, particularly along the coast.

Winter: Coastal rains and possible mudslides along CA-1. Wine country is serene but cool. Be cautious on winding roads.

RV Logistics

Topic	Details
Fueling	Major stations on US-101 and CA-29 cater to diesel rigs. Fuel up before entering CA-1 south of Monterey.
Dump Stations	Located at state parks, county campgrounds, and some vineyards. Napa Valley Expo RV Park offers public access.
Groceries	Full-service markets in Santa Rosa, San Luis Obispo, and Santa Barbara. Stock up inland before Big Sur.
Road Restrictions	Watch for 40-ft vehicle length restrictions along parts of CA-1. Class A rigs often reroute inland.
Cell Coverage	Limited through Big Sur and parts of Mendocino Coast. Download

	maps and campground info in advance.

Suggested Itinerary (10 Days)

Day	Location	Activities
One	Eureka to Mendocino	Redwoods, Avenue of the Giants
Two	Mendocino	Explore headlands and art galleries
Three	Sonoma	Wine tasting, historic plaza
Four	Napa	Hot springs, vineyard tours
Five	San Francisco	Visit city via ferry or shuttle
Six	Half Moon Bay	Beach walk, tidepooling
Seven	Monterey	Aquarium, 17-Mile Drive
Eight	Big Sur	Scenic drive, hiking
Nine	San Simeon	Hearst Castle, elephant seals
Ten	Solvang to Santa	Barbara Wine tasting, oceanfront dining

Drive wisely. Sip slowly. Frequent camping

The California Coast & Wine Country route rewards those who strike a balance between the rush of the road and the pleasure of slowing down. Allow the beat of the waves and the pulse of the vineyards to lead your RV drive, and you'll see why this stretch is still one of America's most famous road trip destinations.

Yellowstone to Glacier Loop

SCAN THE QR CODE

Route Overview

Starting Point: Yellowstone National Park (WY).

Ending Point: Yellowstone National Park (WY) - Full Loop

Total distance: around 850 miles.

Recommended duration is 7-10 days.

Wyoming and Montana

Best travel months are late May to early October (weather allowing).

Route Highlights:

Stop	Key Attractions	RV Facilities
Yellowstone NP	Geysers, Wildlife, Grand Canyon of the Yellowstone	Multiple NPS campgrounds with RV access
Bozeman, MT	Museum of the Rockies, Downtown Arts District	RV parks, fuel, full hookups
Flathead Lake	Waterfront recreation, cherry orchards	State parks and private RV resorts
Glacier NP	Going-to-the-Sun Road, Alpine hikes	Apgar, Fish Creek, and St. Mary campgrounds
Missoula, MT	Breweries, riverfront trails	RV parks, urban amenities
Big Hole Valley	Scenic byway, ghost towns	Rustic camping, boondocking spots

Yellowstone (via West Entrance)	Return via Hebgen Lake	Same as entry point

Segment 1: Yellowstone to Bozeman (around 90 miles)

Exit Yellowstone's north entrance via Gardiner and travel north on US-89. The trip follows the Yellowstone River, where elk and bison often graze along the banks. As you rise toward Livingston, the Absaroka Range dominates the horizon.

Bozeman essentials:

Navigation Tip: Use I-90 west for convenient access.

Points of interest include the Museum of the Rockies (with significant dinosaur displays), Bozeman Hot Springs, and the Gallatin History Museum.

RV Notes: Bozeman Hot Springs Campground is a popular destination for travelers, offering hookups and a direct route to the springs.

Segment 2: Bozeman to Flathead Lake (about 220 miles).

Continue on MT-287 and US-93 for a pastoral drive through expansive Montana valleys. RVers may stop at Butte to see remains of America's mining history before continuing northwest to Flathead Lake, the biggest natural freshwater lake west of the Mississippi.

Flathead Lake essentials:

Tip: Take a detour through Polson for local produce and lakeside dining.

Points of interest include Wild Horse Island (by boat), Flathead Lake State Park, and nearby cherry orchards.

RV Notes: West Shore and Wayfarers state parks provide lakefront campsites with electricity connections and dump facilities.

Segment 3: Flathead Lake to Glacier National Park (about 50 km).

To reach West Glacier, go north on US-93 and then east on US-2. As you approach the crown gem of the Northern Rockies, expect significant elevation changes and twisting roads.

Glacier essentials:

Large RVs are restricted on some stretches of Going-to-the-Sun Road; instead, take a shuttle or park at Apgar or St. Mary.

Points of interest include Lake McDonald, Logan Pass, Hidden Lake Overlook, and Many Glacier.

RV Tip: Make your reservations early—Fish Creek and St. Mary Campgrounds can handle bigger rigs. Generators are permitted during certain hours.

Segment 4: Glacier to Missoula (About 140 miles)

Travel south along US-93, threading through the Flathead Reservation and skirting the Mission Mountains. Missoula is a bustling city with a college-town atmosphere and full-service conveniences.

Missoula essentials:

Navigation Tip: Before 10 a.m., downtown streets are RV-friendly; make early stops for food or supplies.

Attractions include Caras Park, Rattlesnake National Recreation Area, and local craft brewers.

RV Notes: Jellystone Park and Missoula KOA provide a full range of facilities, including propane refills and dog parks.

Segment 5: Missoula to Big Hole Valley (around 130 km)

Follow US-93 south and MT-43 east into the Big Hole Valley—an area marked by wide ranchlands and old routes. This isolated road receives little traffic, giving visitors a natural landscape and isolation.

Big Hole Valley essentials:

Navigation Tip: Fill up before leaving Missoula—services are limited.

Points of interest include Big Hole National Battlefield, Wisdom's antique stores, and ghost town excursions at Bannack State Park.

RV Notes: Primitive sites are available; suitable for self-contained RVs. Excellent stargazing and animal watching.

Segment 6: Return to Yellowstone via West Entrance (about 220 miles).

Descend toward Ennis and Hebgen Lake before looping back into Yellowstone via the West Entrance. The path along MT-287 and US-191 borders rivers and wooded hills, which are often visited by moose and bear.

Final Leg Essentials:

Hebgen Lake is an excellent midway stop for lunch or an overnight stay.

Points of Interest: Earthquake Lake Visitor Center and Madison River fishing locations.

RV Notes: Baker's Hole Campground (just outside the park) has peaceful, first-come, first-served sites with electric connections.

Road Conditions and Safety Notes

Weather: Snow may last until June at higher altitudes; monitor daily predictions, particularly around Glacier.

Fuel: The primary hubs are Bozeman, Missoula, and Polson. Keep tanks at least halfway filled in rural areas.

Cell coverage is limited in both Yellowstone and Glacier. Download offline maps and keep a printed atlas for backup.

Wildlife Caution: There are frequent large-animal crossings; drive conservatively and avoid nighttime driving through park sections.

Insider Planning Tips.

Permits and Passes: The America the Beautiful Pass ($80) provides entrance to both national parks. Book Glacier's car entrance reservation (if necessary) well in advance.

Groceries: Stock up in Bozeman or Missoula. There are limited options in park towns.

Alternative Routes: For additional seclusion, try detouring via the Chief Joseph Scenic Byway or Lolo Pass, both of which are RV-accessible and provide breathtaking vistas.

Summary:

The Yellowstone to Glacier Loop is a bucket-list adventure designed for individuals seeking majesty in the high country and solitude on uncrowded backroads. From scorching geysers and towering peaks to glacier-fed lakes and huckleberry-lined pathways, this journey combines wild nature with well-deserved creature amenities. Thoughtfully spaced locations, excellent RV infrastructure, and an ever-shifting background of natural beauty make this one of the most rewarding circuits in the United States for any RV explorer.

Oregon & Washington Cascades

Overview

The Cascade Range rises like a stone and wood fortress along the spine of Oregon and Washington, anchoring the Pacific Northwest in a stunning environment of volcanic peaks, alpine lakes, lush evergreen forests, and cascading waterfalls. This area is the foundation of one of America's most visually stunning RV roads, excellent for visitors seeking elevation, privacy, and the raw majesty of the wild West.

The Cascades, which straddle the urban border and untamed nature, provide more than simple views. From the snow-covered mountains above Mount Rainier to the lava fields of Mount Bachelor, this route combines outdoor activity, geothermal marvels, and small-town Americana into a one continuous journey. RVers will discover a network of well-maintained routes, convenient campsites, and pullouts suited for large rigs, providing both convenience and immersion.

Key Scenic Routes

1. Cascade Lakes Scenic Byway (Oregon).

Bend to Crescent Junction | Distance: 66 miles.

Elevate your adventure, physically. This byway begins in Bend and rises quickly into Deschutes National Forest, past mirror-clear lakes hidden under volcanic peaks like Mount Bachelor and Broken Top. Ideal for summer and early autumn travel, the road is frequently snowbound from November to May. Numerous Forest Service campsites provide rustic, lakeside overnight accommodations, with trail access only feet from your trailer. Don't miss Sparks Lake at sunset or the volcanic flows around Lava Lake.

2. Mount Hood Scenic Loop (Oregon).

Route: Portland - Mount Hood - Hood River - Portland. Loop: 105 miles

This famous route combines old-growth woods, waterfalls, and the majestic Columbia River. Begin by driving east from Portland on Highway 26. Near Government Camp, Timberline Lodge provides panoramic vistas and a touch of WPA-era architecture. Descend down Highway 35 to fruit-laden Hood River Valley, most brilliant in spring flower and autumn harvest. Return down the Columbia River Gorge, pausing at Multnomah Falls and the Vista House. Several RV-friendly campsites dot the circle, including Trillium Lake, which offers a postcard-worthy vista of Mount Hood.

3. North Cascades Highway (Washington).

Route: Sedro-Woolley to Winthrop via Highway 20 | Distance: 127 miles

This route runs through the isolated North Cascades National Park Complex and is regarded as one of the most challenging and awe-inspiring roads in the United States. Towering granite cliffs, glacial lakes, and wildflower meadows remain constants. The region between Diablo Lake and Washington Pass is very stunning. Facilities are limited, but Colonial Creek Campground provides lakefront RV sites in the center of the woods. Fill up before entering the route, since there are no services for extended periods.

4. Mount Rainier Loop (Washington).

Route: Enumclaw, Sunrise, Paradise, Packwood, and Elbe. Loop: 147 miles.

Circle the famed 14,410-foot stratovolcano on a route brimming with alpine beauty and ancient lodges.

Sunrise, the highest vehicle-accessible point in the park, provides panoramic views of glaciers and flower-filled valleys. In Paradise, waterfalls adorn the slopes and animals roam the meadows. Road gradients are high at spots, and vehicles exceeding 25 feet are urged to approach carefully. Cougar Rock and Ohanapecosh Campgrounds can allow bigger RVs with limited hookups; reservations are highly encouraged.

RV Campgrounds and Key Overnight Stays

Location	Campground	Hookups	Notes
Bend, OR	Tumalo State Park	Full	Riverside setting near Bend; quick access to Scenic Byway
Trillium Lake, OR	Trillium Lake Campground	Dry	Iconic views of Mt. Hood; limited sites, book early
Diablo Lake, WA	Colonial Creek Campground	Dry	Remote but stunning; no hookups, generator hours enforced
Packwood, WA	Cascade Peaks RV Park	Full	All-season access with nearby Mt. Rainier hiking
Leavenworth, WA	Icicle River RV Resort	Full	Bavarian-style town with excellent dining and scenery

Hidden Gems and Worthy Detours.

Newberry Volcanic Monument (OR): This enormous caldera south of Bend has lava tubes, obsidian flows, and twin lakes complete with campers and a small marina.

Stevens Pass Greenway (WA): Connects Puget Sound and Leavenworth via rivers, waterfalls, and traditional logging villages.

Bagby Hot Springs near Mount Hood offers a rustic soak in cedar tubs, while Goldmyer Hot Springs in North Bend provides a lonely thermal paradise (hike-in access).

Winthrop, WA: An Old West-style town in the Methow Valley with wooden boardwalks, unique shops, and riverside dining.

Navigation Tips for RVers

Elevation Changes: Expect regular climbs over 5,000 feet. Ensure that your engine and brakes are in top condition. Use engine braking to avoid overheating.

Winter closures: The North Cascades Highway and Cascade Lakes Scenic Byway are closed seasonally owing to snow. Always check the state DOT's website for current conditions.

Fuel Planning: In hilly terrain, fuel stations might be more than 50 miles apart. Fill up before you reach national forests or picturesque routes.

Connectivity: Cell coverage is often unavailable in the North Cascades and portions of Mount Rainier National Park. Prepare by downloading offline maps and making camping reservations ahead of time.

Best Travel Season

The ideal weather occurs between late June and early October, when roads are clean, campsites are open, and trailheads are easily accessible. Snow lasts until June at higher altitudes, and early snowfall in October may startle the unprepared. Wildflowers bloom in July, and autumn colors illuminate the vine maples and larches from mid-September forward.

Final Thoughts

The Oregon and Washington Cascades reward unhurried driving with majesty best experienced through the broad windows of an RV. From fire-lit lodge evenings to foggy mornings alongside alpine lakes, this area encourages visitors to explore vertically as well as horizontally. Whether following waterfalls or tracking lava flows, RVers will discover that each mile across the Cascades strengthens their connection to the land—and to the adventure itself.

Northwest & Alaska:

Olympic Peninsula Journey

Washington State | Scenic Loop | Approximate distance: 330 miles | Recommended duration: 4-6 days.

Overview

Washington's Olympic Peninsula, bounded by the Pacific Ocean, the Strait of Juan de Fuca, and the Hood Canal, is a region of opposites. Alpine peaks tumble into temperate rainforests, driftwood-strewn beaches along storm-swept cliffs, and moss-laden trees watch over glacier rivers. This route, which makes a roughly clockwise circle along U.S. Route 101, is ideal for RVers looking for quiet, beautiful, and well-spaced service stations. It passes through some of North America's most biodiverse and intriguing environments.

Route Snapshot

Start/End Point: Olympia, Washington

Primary Highway: US-101 Loop

Fuel Access: Reliable throughout the circle; refill before entering National Park inner routes.

Cell coverage is spotty to nonexistent in distant areas—download offline maps.

RV Services: Full hookups in Port Angeles, Forks, and Hoquiam; dry camping is allowed in Olympic National Park.

Road conditions: Mostly paved two-lane with some curves and gradients near mountain passes.

Key Stops and Highlights

1. Olympia to Hoodsport.

Distance: fifty kilometers.
Depart Washington and follow the Hood Canal, a fjord-like waterway with tranquil water vistas and bald eagle sightings. Hoodsport is a worthwhile early stop; stock up, see local wineries, and enjoy Staircase Rapids in Olympic National Park's southeast part.

Don't Miss: Hama Hama Oyster Saloon (fresh seafood straight from the canal).

Glen Ayr Resort offers RV campgrounds with hookups and beachfront access.

2. Lake Cushman and Staircase Wilderness.

Lake Cushman, which branches off from Hoodsport, is a glacier lake surrounded by old-growth forest. The route narrows, but the scenic views reward the careful RV driver. Staircase provides some of the least popular hiking in the park.

Top Hike: Shady Lane Trail (simple loop, river vistas, and mossy woodland).

RV Note: No connections within the park, however basic sites accept rigs under 21-25 feet.

3. Port Angeles and Hurricane Ridge.

Distance: 90 kilometers from Hoodsport.
The city of Port Angeles serves as the regional center, so stock up on supplies, check in at the ranger station, and plan your trip to Hurricane Ridge. On clear days, see across the strait to Canada. The ridge road contains steep gradients and hairpin curves; verify conditions before climbing.

Top Experience: Sunrise at the Hurricane Ridge Visitor Center.

RV campgrounds: Elwha Dam RV Park (full hookups), KOA Port Angeles (amenities, pull-thrus).

4. Sol Duc Valley and Hot Springs.

Distance: 30 miles west of Port Angeles.
This river valley has medicinal waters, cascading waterfalls, and trailheads to the wilderness. RV parking at the Sol Duc Hot Springs Resort is restricted, so come early or stay close.

Don't miss the Sol Duc Falls Trail (0.8 miles, spectacular triple-plunge waterfall).

Camping tip: Sol Duc Campground (no hookups, but can handle RVs up to 35 feet)

5. Forks and the Hoh Rain Forest.

Distance: sixty miles.
Forks, a lumber town, is at the western entry to Olympic National Park's Hoh Rain Forest, which receives more than 140 inches of rain each year. Drive cautiously; animals and elk frequent road shoulders, particularly around dark.

Highlight: The Hall of Mosses Trail (beautiful, primeval woodland, family-friendly).

Local Flavor: Twilight Tour Stops for Pop Culture Fans

RV Stay: Riverview RV Park (peaceful, river-side, full-service).

6. Ruby Beach and Kalaloch Bluffs.

Distance: thirty miles.
Travel south down the coast, passing spectacular beaches surrounded by wooded cliffs. Ruby Beach is a photographer's paradise at low tide, and Kalaloch Lodge provides a handy staging area for cliff top camping and sunset views.

tidal Warning: Always check tidal charts before going beach trekking.

Best RV Site: Kalaloch Campground (no hookups, ocean views, reservable).

7. Lake Quinault Loop.

Distance: forty miles.
The Quinault Rain Forest offers calmer pathways, lakeside seclusion, and antique lodge charm. The Quinault Loop Drive is completely

paved and RV-friendly. Along the journey, see Merriman Falls and the world's largest Sitka spruce.

Recommended Stop: Quinault Mercantile for Last-Minute Supplies.

RV options include Rain Forest Village Resort (limited hookups, lakefront sites).

8. Aberdeen and return to Olympia.

Distance: sixty miles.
Finish your adventure at Aberdeen, a timber town regarded as the entrance to the coast. Before returning to Olympia via US-101, make a grocery stop and relax. Avoid peak travel periods around Shelton.

Road Notes and Navigation Tips

Weather: Coastal parts get fog and unexpected rain year-round. Carry traction devices in shoulder seasons.

Summer traffic might be congested near park gates; leave early and book campsites ahead of time.

Park Pass: Olympic National Park needs a valid America the Beautiful Pass or a daily admission ticket.

Wildlife on the peninsula includes elk, black bears, and mountain goats. Keep food safe and practice Leave No Trace.

Budget Breakdown (Per Day, Couple)

Category	Budget ($)	Mid-Range ($)	Premium ($)
Campground Fees	$20	$45	$90
Fuel (avg 330-mile loop)	$30	$40	$50
Groceries/Dining	$25	$50	$100
Activities & Fees	$10	$25	$40
Daily Total	**$85**	**$160**	**$280**

Insider Detours.

Cape Flattery (Neah Bay) is the northwest point of the contiguous

United States, reachable by SR-112; a Makah Tribe permission is needed.

La Push Beaches: The second and third beaches are a short trek from the parking area; keep an eye out for sneaker waves.

Bogachiel State Park offers a quiet overnight stay with a dense forest canopy.

Final Word

The Olympic Peninsula is more than simply a loop; it's a real, breathing display of nature's richness, all within a reasonable driving distance. For RVers with forethought, flexibility, and a desire to investigate, this voyage offers isolation without surrendering access, as well as untamed beauty without losing comfort.

Idaho Hot Springs Trail

Overview

The Idaho Hot Springs Trail, which winds through rocky wilderness, deep national forests, and lonely alpine basins, is one of the most exciting—and rejuvenating—routes for RV travelers looking for natural thermal springs in unspoiled environs. This one-of-a-kind circle spans over 950 miles, mostly on gravel forest service roads, connecting over 50 natural and developed hot springs across central Idaho. Though it was initially designed as a bikepacking path, its interconnecting access roads provide an intriguing circuit for adventurous RVers, particularly those with Class B rigs, truck campers, or off-road competent setups.

This is not a fast-paced interstate cruise. It's a trek into wilderness seclusion, when cell service is unavailable and time slows down. What's the reward? Granite summits, river valleys, and lodgepole pine forests provide the background to hidden geothermal pools. This path is more than simply hot water; it's also about the journey, the isolation, and the road less traveled.

Route Snapshot

Starting/ending point: Boise, Idaho

Total distance: around 950 miles (loop).

The best time to visit is late June to early October.

Road Type: 70% unpaved woodland roads and 30% paved highways.

Recommended RV types include high-clearance campervans, truck campers, and tiny Class Cs under 25 feet.

Essential Equipment: Paper maps (DeLorme Idaho Atlas or Benchmark), offline GPS, recovery gear, and water purifying equipment.

Major Segments and Hot Spring Highlights
1. Boise to Lowman (by Banks-Lowman Road): 80 miles.

Road Conditions: A paved, meandering mountain road with spectacular overlooks

Key Stops:

Bonneville Hot Springs is a trail-accessible treasure in Warm Springs Creek, with a natural pool close to a cabin remnant.

Kirkham Hot Springs are popular riverbank bathing waters with waterfalls near Lowman, with close parking and rustic camping.

2. Lowman to Stanley (Sawtooth Scenic Byway): 75 km.

Highlights:

Sacajawea Hot Springs: Several rock-lined pools along the river.

Sunbeam Hot Springs is easily accessible from the highway and has warm pools carved into the Salmon River banks.

Overnight options include national forest campsites such as Kirkham, Bonneville, and scattered sites around Redfish Lake.

3. Stanley to Challis (Salmon River Scenic Corridor): 60 km.

Hot Springs on Route:

Challis Hot Springs is developed yet quiet, featuring gravel-bottomed bathing pools and on-site RV campsites (electric connections).

Terrain Notes: Beautiful mountain vistas and river access. Stanley has paved roads but is isolated; stock up on supplies there.

4. Challis to Salmon (Salmon-Challis NF) distance: 60 kilometers.

Soak Spot:

Goldbug Hot Springs is one of Idaho's most photographed natural soaks, with tiered pools and cliff vistas accessible via a hard 2-mile climb.

Caution: Trailhead parking is restricted; come early or camp nearby in scattered areas.

5. Salmon to Elk City (Nez Perce-Clearwater National Forest Backroads)
Distance: 160+ miles.

Conditions: Rugged woodland roads with periodic washboards; high-clearance vehicles advised.

Spring Along the Way:

Jerry Johnson Hot Springs is located off Highway 12, and may be reached by a gorgeous footbridge and a short stroll.

Weir Creek Hot Springs: A quiet woodland spring tucked among mossy boulders.

6. Elk City to McCall (by Warren Wagon Road).
Distance: 190 miles.

Notes: Some areas are small and prone to muck; avoid during rainy conditions. Warren Wagon Road is a seasonal road; consult with the Forest Service before leaving.

Spring of Note:

Burgdorf Hot Springs is a historic resort with rustic charm, chalets, and enormous outdoor pools. RVs may park in surrounding clearings.

Restock Supplies: McCall provides complete facilities and disposal stations.

7. McCall goes to Cascade and returns to Boise.
Distance: 150 miles.

Key Springs:

Gold Fork Hot Springs: Developed but lovely, nestled away in the wilderness with numerous temperature possibilities.

Trail Creek Hot Springs: A popular roadside pool with a mountain view.

Final stretch: Take ID-55 south along the Payette River, returning to Boise via Horseshoe Bend.

Navigation and Safety

Mapping: GPS mapping is problematic in densely wooded regions; carry accurate topographic atlases and route printouts.

gasoline: Some sections surpass 100 miles without services—carry extra gasoline whenever possible.

Water: Most springs are clean, but check temperature and flow conditions. Do not bath if the springs are close to known pollutant sources.

Wildlife: Black bears, moose, and elk are plentiful; keep all food and fragrant things safe when camping.

Fire Restrictions: Always verify the regional fire hazard rating before starting a campfire or using a stove.

Budget Breakdown: Category Average Cost (2 weeks)

Fuel (diesel, gas) $300 - $450
Developed Campgrounds $20-$35 per night.
Dispersed Camping Free Hot Spring entry fees. $0 – $20 (varies)
Supplies & Provisions $200 - $350
An emergency/repair fund of $100 or more is advised.

Pro Tips for RVers

Drive Slowly, Soak Deeply: Unpaved roads need patience. Budget time for pauses, since many of the nicest springs are just a short trek from the trailhead.

Morning Magic: Visit hot springs before morning to see steam rise into the mountain air and sea animals.

Respect the Source: Do not contaminate springs with soap or sunscreen. Many pools support sensitive ecosystems.

Winter Warning: While some developed springs are open year-round, the majority of the trail is inaccessible after the first snowfall. Do not attempt in winter without getting to a single spring via plowed paths.

Notable Side Trips

Frank Church—River of No Return Wilderness: The largest contiguous wilderness in the lower 48; permits are necessary in certain parts.

Sawtooth National Recreation Area: Crystal-clear lakes, jagged peaks, and wildflower meadows. Excellent hiking and stargazing.

McCall's Ponderosa State Park is a lovely lakeside break before finishing the circle.

Final Thoughts

The Idaho Hot Springs Trail is more than just a road trip; it's a geothermal journey into America's vast heartland. With its combination of raw environment and relaxing waterways, it rewards RVers who seek exploration more than haste. Whether soaking solitary beneath a starlit sky or sharing a riverbank pool with other wanderers, this journey provides something rare: a getaway that feels earned.

Keep tires filled, maps dry, and spirits high—Idaho's wild heart awaits.

Explore Montana's Glacier Country Scenic Loop for Waterfalls, Wildlife, and Wilderness.

Alaska Marine Highway & Interior

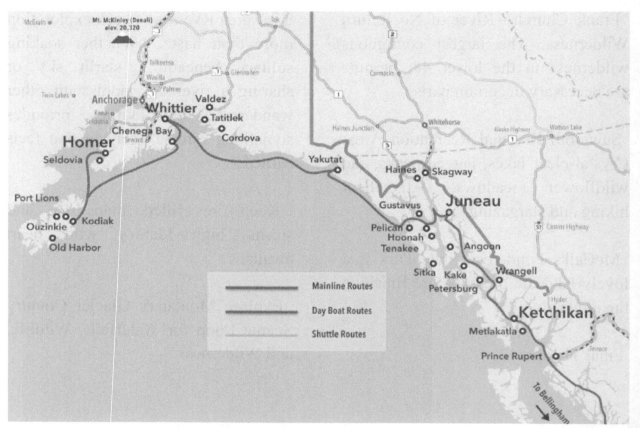

Overview

Alaska's untamed landscape is unlike any other in the United States, rough, isolated, and stunningly huge. Navigating this vast state with an RV demands a combination of smart preparation and a sense of adventure. The Alaska Marine Highway and the state's interior highway system constitute a dynamic partnership, with the former linking coastal settlements via ferry and the latter running deep into the heart of mountainous and tundra territory. Together, they provide unprecedented access to North America's most pristine wilderness.

This section is your route map for both nautical travel and overland adventure. Whether you're island hopping via the Inside Passage or heading north under the midnight sun,

Alaska provides panoramic beauty, animal encounters, and cultural depth—if you know where to look and how to get there.

The Alaska Marine Highway System (AMHS) connects waterborne roads to coastal wilderness.

System Overview

The Alaska Marine Highway is more than just a ferry system; it's a lifeline that connects over 30 coastal villages from Bellingham, Washington, to Dutch Harbor in the Aleutian Chain. For RVers, it serves as a floating freeway, enabling RVs to travel between previously inaccessible coastal spots. It's a crucial route for anybody seeking to avoid the lengthy overland trek across Canada or tour southeast Alaska's island settlements.

Major Ferry Routes For RVers

Bellingham to Haines/Skagway is the gateway route for RVers from the continental United States. It starts in Washington and finishes at the northern panhandle of Alaska. Haines and Skagway are connected to the Alaska Highway, making it an ideal transition point to land-based routes.

Juneau-Sitka-Ketchikan Circuit: These central coastal villages can only be reached by boat or plane. RVers can stay in campgrounds near ferry ports for extended periods of time and explore with local transportation.

Ferries to Kodiak Island and farther west (such as Homer and the Aleutians) are ideal for adventurous RVers seeking secluded places. Be mindful of the inadequate port and road infrastructure in these places.

Vehicle Requirements

Reservations: RV space is limited, so reserve several months in advance during busy summer months.

Size Limits: Take accurate measurements of height, breadth, and length. Some terminals have severe space requirements, such as RVs being under a specific height or length.

Onboard Stays: RV travelers must leave their cars for the journey; arrange to carry necessities inside cabin areas.

Key Tips

Layovers & Logistics: Many RVers break up ferry trips with 1–3 day layovers to tour port communities. Each port has varied connection choices, dump stations, and fuel availability; explore port-specific RV information.

Tide Awareness: Tide levels impact loading ramps; in severe tide zones (such as Cordova), workers may need to readjust during boarding.

Wildlife Spotting: The deck serves as a magnificent viewpoint; bring binoculars to see whales, bald eagles, and sea lions.

Alaska's interior road system: conquering vastness one mile at a time

Mainland Arteries

Alaska's interior highway network may look sparse on a map, yet it is purposefully planned to link major sites while maximizing scenic exposure.

The Alaska Highway (ALCAN) enters Alaska from Yukon in Tok and continues northwest to Delta Junction and Fairbanks. Often considered the primary overland access point for RVers traveling from the Lower 48.

Richardson Highway (AK-4): From Valdez to Fairbanks, this road winds through glacial valleys and rugged landscape, with several pull-offs for photography and overnight camping.

Parks Highway (AK-3) connects Anchorage and Fairbanks to Denali National Park. Well maintained and RV-friendly, this route is ideal for those seeking a blend of accessibility and dramatic scenery.

Tok Cut-Off/Glenn Highway (AK-1): This eastern route connects Tok and Anchorage to Glennallen. Expect mountain vistas and access to Wrangell-St. Elias National Park.

RV Facilities & Fueling

Fuel stations are few outside of big towns. Always fill up at every available station, especially before longer trips like Tok to Glennallen.

Dump Stations: Found in most state-run campsites and private RV parks. Expect fewer amenities than in the Lower 48, and pack extra supplies.

Camping Options: State recreation areas, Bureau of Land Management (BLM) properties, and private RV parks. Outside municipal boundaries, boondocking is normally legal; nevertheless, check for wildlife cautions.

Notable Stops and Side Routes

1. Tok

The unofficial welcoming point for overland visitors to Alaska. It has an RV-friendly tourist center, tire repair businesses, and overnight camping.

2. Fairbanks.

Northern hub with comprehensive service. Visit the Museum of the North, Chena Hot Springs, and consider continuing to the Dalton Highway, a difficult, gravel path to the Arctic Circle (not recommended for inexperienced RVers or trailers).

3. Denali National Park.

Riley Creek Campground has a limited number of RV sites accessible near the park's entrance. Private shuttles and the Denali Park Road bus service provide access to interior wildlife viewing.

4) Glennallen

The gateway to America's biggest national park, Wrangell-St. Elias. While a tow vehicle is required to enter the interior, the journey via Richardson and Nabesna Roads is rewarding in terms of glaciers and hiking chances.

5. Valdez

Located at the head of a deep fjord, surrounded by mountains and waterfalls. A picturesque terminus or rest station with boat service to Whittier.

6. Kenai Peninsula.

The Seward Highway connects Anchorage to Seward. This area is known for its superb fishing, beautiful coastal vistas, and family-friendly RV parks in cities like Homer, Seward, and Soldotna.

Seasonal considerations

Summer (May-September) is the peak travel season. Long daylight hours (up to 20+ hours), most ferry lines operational, and full camping capacity.

Spring and fall: Roads remain open, but ferry service becomes irregular. Some campsites shut after Labor Day.

Winter: Extreme weather, decreased service. Some routes (like Dalton) remain open but are designed for well-equipped trucks only. Ferry routes may operate with skeleton schedules.

Final Navigation Notes

GPS Caution: GPS systems may misroute passengers or mislabel routes. Always carry a printed or digital offline road map for Alaska.

Wildlife Hazards: Moose and bears regularly cross roadways. Avoid driving at night.

Connectivity: Cell signal is unreliable throughout the interior. Satellite communication systems and CB radios are suggested for emergency preparation.

In Alaska, the trip is as important as the goal itself. Whether traveling the seaside routes aboard the AMHS or traversing the ridgelines of the vast Interior, RVers ready to accept the state's vastness and seclusion will discover a road map that leads to unrivaled adventure.

Chapter 5: RV-Friendly National Parks

Top 20 RV-Accessible National Parks

From Alpine Peaks to Desert Wonders: Explore America's Most RV-Friendly Natural Treasures

The United States is a wide canvas of ecosystems, monuments, and protected wilderness, allowing RV travelers to experience nature's masterpieces with unprecedented freedom. The following twenty national parks are notable not just for their spectacular landscape, but also for their infrastructure, accessibility, and inviting facilities for recreational vehicles of all sizes. Whether you're looking for waterfalls, red rock canyons, coastal roads, or alpine lakes, these parks are great starting points for amazing road trips.

1. Yellowstone National Park — Wyoming, Montana, Idaho
Best for geysers, animals, and geothermal marvels.
RV tips: There are several campsites that accommodate RVs up to 40 feet. Fishing Bridge RV Park (full hookups) is a popular option,

although it sells out months in advance. Roads might be limited in certain areas; verify seasonal restrictions.

Highlight Drive: The Grand Loop Road has 142 miles of geysers, hot springs, and bison sightings.

2. Grand Teton National Park, Wyoming.

Ideal for: rugged peaks, alpine lakes, and picturesque byways.

RV Tip: Colter Bay RV Park has full hookups and lake views. Gros Ventre Campground can handle bigger rigs.

Highlight Drive: Teton Park Road, particularly around daybreak, provides spectacular vistas of the Tetons.

3. Zion National Park in Utah is ideal for exploring sandstone cliffs, canyons, and adventurous treks.

RV Tips: South and Watchman Campgrounds both welcome RVs, with Watchman offering electric connections. Most of the year, Zion Canyon Scenic Drive is only accessible via shuttle.

Highlight Drive: Kolob Canyons Road—no shuttle needed and RV compatible.

4. Acadia National Park – Maine

Ideal for: Coastal cliffs, fall foliage, and rocky beaches.

RV Tip: The Blackwoods and Seawall Campgrounds accommodate most RVs; however, there are no hookups. Private parks nearby provide full service.

Highlight Drive: Park Loop Road has pull-offs suitable for photography and short walks.

5. Glacier National Park – Montana

Ideal for: Alpine scenery and glacier valleys.

RV tips: Due to size restrictions, larger rigs are unable to go past Avalanche on the Going-to-the-Sun Road. St. Mary and Apgar Campgrounds welcome RVs, and some even provide generator hours.

Highlight Drive: Drive as far as is permissible on Going-to-the-Sun, then take the shuttle or a towed car.

6. Great Smoky Mountains National Park, Tennessee & North Carolina.

Best for: Forested mountains, historical buildings, and animals.

RV Tip: Cades Cove and Elkmont Campgrounds allow RVs. There are no hookups at the park, but numerous neighboring choices include full-service RV parks.

Highlight Drive: The Cades Cove Loop, an 11-mile history tour with regular bear sightings.

7. Bryce Canyon National Park in Utah is ideal for exploring hoodoos, high desert plateaus, and stargazing.

RV Tips: RVs are permitted in the North and Sunset campgrounds. Sunset Campground has several pull-throughs. No connections, but trash stations and potable water are accessible.

Highlight Drive: The Bryce Amphitheater Scenic Drive has significant overlooks such as Sunrise, Sunset, and Inspiration Point.

8. Rocky Mountain National Park – Colorado

Ideal for: Alpine tundra, elk herds, and snow capped summits.

RV Tips: Moraine Park and Glacier Basin Campgrounds may handle bigger rigs but do not provide connections. Trail Ridge Road may be steep; verify conditions before traversing it.

Highlight drive: Trail Ridge Road, North America's highest continuous paved road (seasonal).

9. Yosemite National Park, California.

Ideal for: waterfalls, granite cliffs, and valley vistas.

RV Tip: Lower Pines and North Pines Campgrounds can accommodate RVs up to 40 feet. There are no connections in the park; bring solar or a generator.

Highlight Drive: Tioga Road (summer) provides wonderful access to the high country.

10. Arches National Park in Utah is known for its stunning natural arches and red rock formations.

RV tips: Devils Garden Campground can accommodate RVs up to 40 feet. No connections. The roads are well-paved and accessible to most RVs.

Highlight the Arches Scenic Drive to Windows Section and Delicate Arch perspectives.

11. Joshua Tree National Park – California

Ideal for: desert vistas, climbing, and starry nights.

RV Tips: Black Rock and Cottonwood Campgrounds provide RV access but no hookups and minimal water. Summer temperatures rise; come from October to April.

Highlight Drive: Park Boulevard connects the Mojave and Colorado deserts.

12. Badlands National Park, South Dakota.

Best for eroded buttes, fossil beds, and broad plains.

RV Tips: Cedar Pass Campground accommodates bigger RVs and has electric sites. The roads are broad and flat.

Highlight Drive: Badlands Loop Road (Highway 240) has scenic vistas and short treks.

13. Olympic National Park – Washington

Ideal for: rainforests, beaches, and alpine ranges.

RV Tips: Sol Duc, Kalaloch, and Hoh Campgrounds accept RVs, although size limits apply. No connections, however neighboring private choices are available.

Highlight Drive: Hurricane Ridge Road provides mountain vistas and accessible RV parking spaces.

14. Sequoia and Kings Canyon National Parks, California

Ideal for giant trees, mountain roads, and deep valleys.

RV Tips: Lodgepole Campground can accommodate RVs up to 40 feet. Be cautious on tight, curving roads. Generators are only operational during particular hours.

Highlight Drive: Generals Highway—an renowned drive through towering sequoia trees.

15. Grand Canyon National Park – Arizona

Best for: Canyon panoramas, sunrises, and Colorado River views.

RV Tip: Trailer Village at the South Rim is the only in-park option that offers full hookups. The Desert View Campground is more rustic and picturesque.

Highlight Drive: Desert View Drive—less congested than the Village and with several vistas.

16. Death Valley National Park, California and Nevada

Ideal for: salt flats, sand dunes, and spectacular geology.

RV Tip: Furnace Creek Campground has full hookups, while some provide dry camping. Come prepared—this is the hottest area in North America.

Highlight Drive: Badwater Road to Artist's Drive—vibrant desert color schemes.

17. Shenandoah National Park – Virginia

Ideal for: Blue Ridge Parkway access and wooded ridgelines.

RV Tip: Big Meadows and Loft Mountain Campgrounds are

RV-friendly. There are no connections, however disposal stations are provided.

Highlight Drive: Skyline Drive, which covers 105 kilometers and has 75 views.

18. Capitol Reef National Park in Utah is ideal for exploring fruit orchards, canyons, and seclusion. RV Tips: Fruita Campground can accommodate RVs up to 52 feet. Limited amenities; come self-contained.

Highlight Drive: The scenic drive to Capitol Gorge and Grand Wash.

19. Big Bend National Park – Texas

Best for desert seclusion, canyons, and vistas of the Rio Grande.

RV Tips: Rio Grande Village RV Campground offers full hookups, but the basic sites need dry camping skills.

Ross Maxwell Scenic Drive highlights the Chisos Mountains and Santa Elena Canyon.

20. Lassen Volcanic National Park, California.

Ideal for: Hydrothermal characteristics, volcanic summits, and isolation.

RV Tips: Manzanita Lake Campground accommodates big rigs

and has some utilities. The Lassen Volcanic Highway is well-maintained, however there are some steep stretches.

Highlight Drive: The Lassen Volcanic National Highway links all key sights in a picturesque circle.

Key Navigation Advice

Size Matters: Always check the maximum vehicle length regulations for campers and picturesque routes.

Book early: RV-accessible campsites at national parks are often booked 6-12 months in advance.

Generators and Hookups: Many parks restrict generator hours and do not provide hookups—bring enough battery power, solar, or water.

Seasonal Closures: Snow may obstruct access to higher altitudes from late autumn to spring; check NPS notifications before going.

Whether parked next to old trees or along a canyon rim, these parks provide unparalleled natural immersion while keeping you comfortable in your RV. The perfect mix of planning and route selection transforms your national park visit into a smooth, breathtaking experience.

Reservation Tips & Park Regulations

Navigating America's extensive network of campsites and RV parks needs more than just a sense of direction; it also necessitates planning, timing, and knowledge with a constantly changing world of reservation systems and laws. Whether you park among redwood giants, along the lip of the Grand Canyon, or at a coastal Florida state park, your experience is determined by how well you plan. This book explains the most important techniques and laws that RVers should be aware of in order to remain one step ahead and in compliance throughout the 2025 travel season.

Reservation System Decoded

The demand for RV-friendly campsites has skyrocketed, and being spontaneous is no longer a guarantee of success, particularly during peak seasons or in popular national destinations. Many campsites now accept reservations exclusively, with rolling booking periods that vary by system and location.

Key Platforms to Know:

Recreation.gov covers federal areas such as National Parks, Forest Service locations, the Bureau of Land Management (BLM), and the Army Corps of Engineers. Booking windows typically open six months in advance, at 10:00 a.m. Eastern Time. Popular places may sell out in minutes.

ReserveAmerica: A common platform for many state parks in the United States, although not universal. Each state has its own lead time, which ranges from three to eleven months.

State-specific portals: California, Texas, and Florida have their own booking systems. Before creating a regional route, get to know each of them.

Private campgrounds (Koa, Good Sam, etc.) often accept bookings up to a year in advance. These sites often provide greater facilities and cancellation options, but at a higher nightly charge.

Best Practices For Booking Success

Know the window.

Mark down the first day of reservation availability on your calendar and book as soon as the clock strikes. To reserve spaces at prominent attractions, make reminders and utilize several devices.

Flexible travel dates

Midweek arrivals and shoulder-season travel (April-May, September-October) provide the most availability and a calmer environment.

Backup Options

Popular campgrounds may not permit rigs longer than a particular length or may lack connections. Keep alternatives, such as adjacent private campers, on your schedule.

Are you ready to go off-grid?

Dispersed camping on national forests and BLM lands is frequently free but without services. Make sure your rig is self-contained, with enough water, waste storage, and power capacity.

Park Entry and Length Restrictions

Vehicle length restrictions may apply in national and state parks due to small roads, tight curves, or old campsite layouts. Before you arrive, check the park's individual restrictions. This is a broad guide:

Park Type: Max RV Length Allowed: Older National Parks: 25-30 feet Modern State Parks: 35-40 feet Private RV Resorts: 45 feet or more (Big Rig Friendly)

Height clearance is also critical, especially in Eastern parks where low bridges, tunnels, and tree canopies might cause issues. Always use your RV's precise measurements when planning itineraries and reservations.

Permit and Pass Systems

Some places now demand more permissions than just campsite bookings. Others utilize timed-entry systems to manage traffic and safeguard sensitive areas.

Timed entrance Passes: During peak season, parks such as Rocky Mountain, Arches, and Glacier offer car entrance reservations. These are normally maintained via Recreation.gov and are distinct from campsite reservations.

Annual Passes: The America the Beautiful Pass ($80) covers admission costs to over 2,000 federal recreation areas and may pay for itself in just a few trips.

State Park Passes: If you plan to explore extensively within a particular area, consider purchasing a state-specific yearly pass (for example, the California Explorer Pass or the Texas State Parks Pass).

Campsite Etiquette and Regulations

Compliance with campground rules ensures that these treasured spaces remain safe, comfortable, and sustainable. Park guards and hosts rigorously enforce standards; violations might result with penalties or eviction.

Core Rules Nationwide:

Check-in and check-out times are typically 12:00 p.m. or 1:00 p.m., and 10:00 a.m. or 11:00 a.m., respectively. Early comers may be turned away.

Generator hours are limited to certain times (e.g., 8-10 a.m., 4-6 p.m.) to ensure calm hours.

Campfires: Only permitted in specified rings; subject to seasonal limits due to wildfire danger. Always check the current fire regulations.

Pets must always be on a leash. Some paths or beaches may prohibit dogs completely. Clean-up is required.

Waste disposal: Most established campsites include dump facilities. Illegal dumping is strictly forbidden and severely fined.

Stay Limits: Maximum durations are often regulated (e.g., 14 consecutive days) to guarantee equitable access. Extensions are unusual.

When Plans Change: Know the Cancellation Policies
Each reservation platform has its own canceling policies:

Recreation.gov: Modifications or cancellations submitted at least two days in advance are normally refunded, less a nominal charge.

Penalties in state parks differ. Some jurisdictions allow partial refunds up to 24 hours before arrival, while others need a longer notice.

Private Parks: Policies are often more forgiving, but check the small print, particularly during holidays or events.

Weather, mechanical issues, and last-minute changes are all part of RV life. Always read the cancellation policy before confirming a reservation to avoid unnecessary losses.

The Bottom Line

The fine print reveals where the freedom of the open road meets reality. Smart RVers thrive not simply through wanderlust, but also by dedication, early preparation, and a thorough understanding of the processes that influence where and how you park for the night. The finest excursions begin with knowing where you're going and what's expected when you arrive.

Navigating Narrow Roads & Height Limits

Know Before You Go: Understanding Road Restrictions

Traveling by RV allows you to experience the freedom of the open road, but it also brings unique problems, the most notable of which being road width limits and overhead clearance limitations. Unlike passenger cars, RVs need a greater understanding of physical measurements and road categories. An apparently picturesque byway may rapidly become dangerous if it passes via a covered bridge or winds around cliffside switchbacks with little space to drive.

To drive intelligently in 2025, you must first understand how the United States' infrastructure handles heavy cars. Not all roads are created equally. From small colonial alleyways in New England to serpentine canyon passes in the West, America's unique geography needs meticulous planning. Height, breadth, and weight regulations are enforced for safety and preservation, and infractions may result in significant fines—or worse, structural damage to your rig.

Width Awareness: Narrow Lanes and Backroads

Most Class A, B, and C RVs are 7.5 to 8.5 feet wide (excluding mirrors), which is close to the federal limit of 8.5 feet on interstates and major highways. However, many rural or historic roads, particularly those in older cities or hilly areas, were not constructed for contemporary recreational vehicles.

Key signals to heed include:

"No Trucks" or "No Oversized Vehicles": This indicates a possible problem with lane width or clearance. Typically found in residential areas or near historic neighborhoods.

"One-Lane Road Ahead": May be manageable for automobiles but difficult for RVs, particularly if there is no turnaround.

"Sharp Curves": This is especially true in the Smoky Mountains, Appalachians, and coastal highways such as California's Highway 1, where

guardrails may be few and shoulders non-existent.

Pro Tip: Use RV-specific GPS systems or apps for lane direction, clearance alerts, and real-time diversions. Unlike normal navigation systems, they take into consideration your vehicle's specific measurements.

Height clearance: avoiding the dreaded bridge strike.

One of the most significant metrics for any RVer is height—the distance from the ground to the tallest permanent point on your trailer. The typical RV height is between 10 and 13.5 feet. Federal rules require interstate overpasses to have a minimum clearance of 14 feet, although non-interstate highways may descend significantly lower.

Key height thresholds:

The standard minimum for US interstate overpasses is 14 feet.

12-13 feet: Common in older cities, state highways, and minor roads.

Below 12 feet: Common on parkways, tunnels, and rural roads in the Northeast (particularly New York and Pennsylvania).

Low clearance marks are generally displayed well in advance, although not necessarily in obvious spots—especially in older cities or underpasses maintained by local administrations. Ignoring them might result in expensive accidents and trip-ending delays.

Crucial Avoidance Zones:

No commercial or big vehicles are allowed on New York's parkway system, particularly the Hutchinson River Parkway and the Southern State Parkway.

Downtown Boston and Philadelphia: Tight curves, low bridges, and weight-restricted tunnels abound.

Lower Wacker Drive in Chicago is made up of many layers of roadways with differing clearance levels.

Weight and Width Restrictions: Overlooked Obstacles

Bridge weight limitations are often stated just before crossing, providing little time for other routes. Always be aware of your vehicle's Gross Vehicle Weight Rating (GVWR) and avoid highways with tonnage limitations. Pay great attention to seasonal weight limitations in northern regions, especially during spring thaw when roads are prone to high loads.

Monitor bridge and road classifications:

"Weight Limit 5 Tons" is a frequent limitation in rural regions with aging infrastructure.

"No Vehicles Over 20 ft": This applies to narrow switchbacks or roads with limited turn radii.

"Truck Route" signs: Follow them, since they often go around unsuitable routes for heavier cars.

Tools of the Trade: Plan with Precision.
Avoid relying entirely on paper maps or general-purpose GPS. Navigation systems designed specifically for RVs are your first line of defense against unexpected clearances and route changes. Consider the following tools.

Garmin RV Series GPS Units: Customized to your vehicle specifications.

RV LIFE Trip Wizard: Provides extensive planning, road grade information, and customizable alarms.

LowClearances.com is a frequently updated database of identified dangers in the United States.

State DOT Websites: Many states include interactive maps that display construction, limitations, and alternate truck-friendly routes.

Real-World Example: Preventing a Classic Mistake

Imagine driving through North Carolina's picturesque Blue Ridge Parkway, entranced by the magnificent vistas, only to come upon a stone bridge measuring 11'4" with no shoulder or turning. For many people, this is the point at which their dreams turn into nightmares. However, with extensive route vetting and real-time navigation capabilities, it is completely preventable.

Final Checklist for Dimensions, Data, and Diligence

Before every journey:

Measure your rig, including rooftop attachments, and mark it near your dashboard.

Input your measurements into your GPS: And ensure that height and weight notifications are enabled.

Scanning your route ahead of time is especially important while going on new or picturesque byways.

Check for DOT updates: Seasonal roadwork or new signs might render a previously safe route unsuitable.

Carry a paper atlas. As a failsafe in areas with poor signal or device failure.

In the world of RV travel, preparedness equals freedom. When you consider the vertical and lateral constraints of America's highways, the whole highway system opens up with confidence. With the correct information and skills, even the smallest road becomes part of the journey, rather than a detour into tragedy.

Chapter 6: Hidden Gems Off the Beaten Path

Underrated State Parks

Explore the Unsung Natural Wonders of the USA.

Beyond the well-traveled pathways of Yellowstone, Yosemite, and the Great Smoky Mountains, America's state parks provide a calmer, more personal encounter with nature. These landscapes—less commercialized, more accessible, and rich in regional character—are great for RV travelers seeking peace, tranquility, and breathtaking grandeur away from the throng. This section features a handpicked selection of underappreciated state parks that need to be on every road warrior's itinerary. From alpine lakes to desert canyons, coastal woodlands to prairie panoramas, each location offers unique chances for exploration, relaxation, and rejuvenation—often with full RV hookups and less reservations necessary.

1. Custer State Park, South Dakota
Why Go:

Custer State Park, a 71,000-acre jewel in the Black Hills, is sometimes overshadowed by adjacent Mount Rushmore and Badlands National Park. Winding scenic highways like Needles Highway and Iron Mountain Road provide breathtaking views of granite spires, deep pine woods, and free-roaming bison herds—one of the biggest publicly owned in the nation.

RV Tips: Blue Bell and Game Lodge campgrounds have full hookups and contemporary facilities, and are conveniently located near fishing, hiking, and wildlife-viewing trails. Roads may be narrow and curvy, so use a tow vehicle or a smaller Class C RV.

Custer State Park

2. Valley of Fire State Park, Nevada
Why Go:
This strange red rock terrain, about an hour from Las Vegas, surpasses any national park for geological drama. The sandstone formations shine brightly in the Nevada sun, revealing ancient petroglyphs, slot

canyons, and picturesque paths with little foot traffic.

RV Tips: Atlatl Rock and Arch Rock campsites may accommodate RVs up to 35 feet. However, spots are limited, so arrive early, particularly during colder months. There are no connections, but trash stations and water are accessible. Solar panels flourish here.

Valley of Fire State Park

3. Goblin Valley State Park, Utah
Reasons to Visit:
Tucked between Capitol Reef and Canyonlands National Parks, Goblin Valley is a strange, otherworldly desert with hoodoos and "goblins"—soft sandstone structures carved by millennia of wind and

water. It's a haven for families and photographers.

RV Tips: On-site campground has electric connections and spacious pull-through sites. The park is secluded, so stock up on petrol and supplies before you arrive. Cell service is restricted; download maps in advance.

Goblin Valley State Park

4. Myakka River State Park, Florida
Why go:
This large subtropical park east of Sarasota provides a refreshing contrast to Florida's congested coastlines. Slow-moving blackwater rivers meander through marshes and grasslands filled with alligators, wading birds, and old-growth oak hammocks.

RV Tips: Three parks fit all RV sizes and provide power and water connections under shaded canopies. Canoe and airboat rentals allow you to explore the rivers, which are ideal for getting away from the asphalt.

Myakka River State Park,

5. Porcupine Mountains Wilderness State Park, Michigan.
Why go:
Michigan's biggest state park borders the beaches of Lake Superior and is covered with old-growth hardwood forest. The mountainous landscape is defined by dramatic ridgelines, waterfalls in the backcountry, and panoramic vistas of lakes. In the autumn, this is one of the Midwest's top foliage locations.

RV Tips: Union Bay Campground has contemporary facilities including electricity and convenient access to Lake Superior's beach. Due to severe winters, the park runs seasonally; confirm access before coming north.

6. Dead Horse Point State Park, Utah
Why Go:

Located just outside Moab, this mesa-top park provides panoramic views of the Colorado River and Canyonlands National Park. It's an excellent dawn and sunset watching area, with views that equal those of national parks—minus the jams.

RV Tips: Kayenta and Wingate parks have asphalt RV spaces, electricity hookups, and WiFi. During high season, sites book rapidly, so make your reservations early. The park is designated as having a dark sky, making it perfect for astronomy.

7. Gooseberry Falls State Park, Minnesota
Why go:
Crashing waterfalls, basalt cliffs, and lush birch woods characterize this North Shore treasure on Lake Superior's border. It's a tranquil getaway near Duluth that combines watery fun with boreal forest splendor.

RV Tips: RV-friendly sites with power connections are available all year. The main campsite is a short walk from the falls and the tourist center. Bugs might be abundant in the summer; bring repellents and nets.

8. Anza-Borrego Desert State Park, California.
Why go:
California's biggest state park has 600,000 acres of badlands, wildflower valleys, and slot canyons. During the spring, the desert blossoms with color, drawing both nature lovers and RVers looking for peace and quiet.

RV Tips: Borrego Palm Canyon Campground has both full and partial hookups. Boondocking is permitted in numerous designated places across the park—ideal for self-sufficient RVs. Summer temperatures climb; plan trips from autumn to spring.

9. Cloudland Canyon State Park, Georgia
Why go:
Perched atop Lookout Mountain, Cloudland Canyon reveals vast canyons, sandstone cliffs, and flowing waterfalls. It's one of the Southeast's

best-kept secrets for mountain views and hiking.

RV Tips: Two campsites provide full-service hookups and access to trails. The roads are steep and winding—be cautious on the approach, particularly with larger trucks. A towed vehicle is useful for exploring the surroundings.

10. Caprock Canyons State Park, Texas Why Go:

This rugged West Texas refuge, sometimes overlooked in favor of Palo Duro, is home to red-rock canyons, high grasslands, and a free-roaming bison herd. Trails vary from moderate walks to difficult scrambles along canyon walls.

RV Tips: Water and power connections are available near the visitor center. Summer heat may be harsh; opt for shoulder seasons. Bring extra water and make sure your rig's cooling systems are in peak condition.

Pro Tip for Visiting Underrated State Parks: Reserve in advance. Although less busy, many state parks still need previous reservations, particularly for RV hookups.

Before traveling, check for restrictions such as road grades, vehicle length limitations, and seasonal closures.

Go Midweek: Weekends fill up quickly, while weekdays provide a better site selection and more solitude.

Mind Connectivity: Many parks have limited cell service, so download offline maps and campground information ahead of time.

Pack Sufficiently: Smaller parks sometimes have fewer facilities than national parks, so bring water, gasoline, and supplies.

These hidden treasures are not only picturesque, but also strategically dispersed throughout the country, making them perfect for putting together a coast-to-coast RV itinerary full of quiet moments, real discoveries, and natural majesty that people who follow the main road frequently miss. Allow the undervalued to become remembered on your 2025 journey.

Small Town America with Big Charm

Small villages that pulse with a quiet type of charm may be found all throughout the United States, snuggled between mountain ranges, tucked into wooded valleys, and along seaside backroads. These aren't the flashy cities with soaring skylines, but rather the locations where porches creak with character, eateries still offer pie à la mode with a wink, and strangers greet like old friends. For RV travelers, these villages provide a slower pace, real connection, and a welcome respite from the bustle of the road.

This section details a chosen selection of small-town jewels around the nation, each with its own personality, historical significance, and RV-friendly appeal. Whether you're attracted to old stores, offbeat festivals, or the frontier spirit, these sites beg you to slow down and park for a bit.

Northeast: Colonial Charm and Maritime Whimsy.

Woodstock, Vermont's population is 3,000.

Why Go: Covered bridges, autumn foliage, and restored 18th-century buildings.

RV Tip: Stay at the Quechee/Pine Valley KOA for easy access to trails and artisan stores.

Highlight: The Billings Farm & Museum provides a genuine piece of rural tradition, replete with Jersey cows and butter churning demonstrations.

Mystic, CT
Population: 4,200.

Why Visit: Maritime history meets seaside attractiveness.

RV Tip: Seaport Campground is conveniently located near the famous Mystic Seaport Museum and downtown.

Highlight: Go to B.F. Clyde's Cider Mill, America's oldest steam-powered cider mill.

South: Southern hospitality and timeless traditions.

Fairhope, Alabama
Population: 23,000

Why Visit: Bluffs overlooking Mobile Bay and a thriving cultural scene.

RV Tip: Coastal Haven RV Park has well-shaded areas and fresh seafood nearby.

Highlight: Take a stroll along the Fairhope Pier after sunset and listen to local musicians perform in neighboring parks.

Mount Airy, NC
Population: 10,300.

Why Visit: The real-life inspiration for Mayberry from The Andy Griffith Show.

RV Tip: Mayberry Campground captures the town's charm with themed décor and convenient access to the main strip.

Highlight: Visit the Andy Griffith Museum and enjoy a live bluegrass concert at the historic Earle Theatre.

Midwest: Americana Heartbeats and Heritage Towns.

Galena, Illinois
Population: 3,200.

Why Go: 19th-century stores, Civil War-era residences, and cobblestone streets.

RV Tip: Palace Campgrounds has full hookups only minutes from downtown.

Highlight: Visit Ulysses S. Grant's residence and browse the antique stores that line Main Street.

Lanesboro, Minnesota
Population: 730.
Why Go: Bicycles, bed & breakfasts, and cliffs along the Root River Trail.
RV Tip: Stay at Eagle Cliff Campground for riverside sites and kayaking.
Highlight: The town serves as a magnet for theater enthusiasts; don't miss a performance at the Commonweal Theatre.

West: Frontier Spirit and Rugged Beauty.
Wallace, Idaho
Population: 800.
Why Visit: The silver mining tradition has been maintained with a vivid flare.
Wallace RV Park is located along the river and is easily accessible to saloons and museums on foot.
Highlight: Take the Sierra Silver Mine Tour by trolley and hear anecdotes from past miners.

Silverton, Colorado has a population of 600.
Why Go: High-altitude scenery and Wild West origins.
RV Tip: Red Mountain RV Park has breathtaking views and access to the San Juan Skyway.

Highlight: Take the Durango & Silverton Narrow Gauge Railroad for an incredible panoramic ride.

Pacific Northwest & California: Eccentric Finds and Nature's Bounty

Jacksonville, Oregon
Population: 3,000.
Why Go: Gold Rush echoes mingle with modern-day vineyards and events.
RV Tip: Valley of the Rogue State Park is a short drive away and follows the river.
Highlight: Attend the summer Britt Music Festival, held in a hillside amphitheater beneath the stars.

Solvang, Calif.
Population: 6,000.
Why Go: A taste of Denmark in the Santa Barbara wine region.
RV Tip: Flying Flags. The RV Resort in neighboring Buellton combines luxury with facilities such as fire pits and pools.
Highlight: Try (Danish pancake balls) at one of the numerous bakeries.

Southwest: Desert Bloom and Artistic Spirit.

Madrid, NM

Population: 200.

Why Go: An ancient coal town has been revived as an unusual artist community.

RV Tip: Stay at Rancheros de Santa Fe RV Park and enjoy the picturesque journey along the Turquoise Trail.

Highlights include seeing eccentric galleries and then enjoying a green chile cheeseburger at the Mine Shaft Tavern.

Jerome, Arizona has a population of 450.

Why Go: A deserted hamlet turned bohemian haven nestled atop Cleopatra Hill.

RV Tip: Verde Valley RV & Camping Resort serves as a base for exploring Cottonwood, Sedona, and Jerome.

Highlight: Don't miss the Jerome State Historic Park, which tells stories of copper, collapse, and revival.

Tips for Exploring Small-Town America by RV

Respect Local Rhythm: Many small communities move at a slower pace. Avoid peak hours, follow established parking laws, and enjoy calm talks.

Support Local Businesses: Visit mom-and-pop stores, local grocers, and roadside markets. Every dollar helps to preserve the town's distinct charm.

Stay off the Freeway: Scenic byways like the Great River Road and Blue Ridge Parkway provide more personal access to small-town gems.

Plan Ahead, But Not Too Much: Although many RV sites accept reservations, tiny communities often value spontaneity. Allow a few nights for unforeseen diversions.

Accept the Odd: Whether it's a squirrel statue festival, a sock museum, or the world's biggest rocking rocker, tiny communities thrive at the unique.

Final Thought

Small-town America is not a side trip; it is an important part of your RV travel. These villages weave together history, culture, and community spirit. They're locations where the coffee is strong, the neighbors are interested, and the air has a slight aroma of firewood and new breeds. Allow your atlas to lead you off the usual road and into the heart of the country, one delightful town at a time.

Unique Festivals & Local Eats

Celebrate the Spirit of America! One bite and event at a time.

The United States provides a vivid tapestry of regional flavor and festivity, from agriculturally rich county fairs to eccentric neighborhood festivities and culinary festivals that pique your taste senses. For RV visitors, these events provide an unrivaled chance to connect with locals, support small-town economies, and sample genuine food that seldom appears on major menus. This section lists noteworthy yearly events by area, providing a personalized schedule of where to go, what to eat, and when to get there—all geared to the freedom of a mobile lifestyle.

Northeast USA

Vermont Maple Festival, St. Albans, VT (Late April)

As sap season approaches, this quaint celebration honors Vermont's tastiest product. Explore sugarhouse demonstrations, sample maple-infused treats (from cotton candy to BBQ ribs), and shop for artisan goods in the historic downtown. RV parking is offered at Lake Carmi State Park, a picturesque base with hookups and fire rings.

Maine Lobster Festival - Rockland, Maine (Early August)

Over 20,000 pounds of lobster are served over five days, including rolls, steaming feasts, and lobster ice cream. The harborfront carnival atmosphere includes sea goddess coronations, marine parades, and trap-hauling competitions. Snow Marine Park is ideal for dry camping, whereas Camden Hills State Park has complete RV facilities.

Southeast USA

National Cornbread Festival - South Pittsburg, Tennessee (Late April)

Celebrate the cast-iron history at America's Lodge Cookware Capital. The Cornbread Alley offers a variety of cornbread flavors, including jalapeño-cheddar and peach cobbler, along with live bluegrass music and cast-iron pan competitions. The Tennessee River offers gorgeous boondocking possibilities, while Marion County Park has full-service RV sites.

Shrimp and Grits Festival - Jekyll Island, Georgia (Mid-September)

This exquisite beachside event highlights a Lowcountry staple. Sample hundreds of shrimp-and-grits variations from chefs around the Southeast while enjoying island music, art booths, and beach vistas. The nearest RV-friendly alternative is the Jekyll Island Campground, which is covered by live oaks and has hookups and a basic shop.

Midwest USA

Tulip Time Festival - Holland, Michigan (Early May)

Over six million flowering tulips provided a background for Dutch heritage parades, wooden shoe dances, and stroopwafel tastings. While touristic, this event is well-organized, with shuttle-accessible RV parking at the neighboring fairgrounds and full-service campsites at Holland State Park on Lake Michigan.

Pierogi Fest - Whiting, Indiana (late July)

Polish-American pride comes through at this charmingly unique festival. Expect pierogi with whatever filling you can think of—potato-cheddar, sauerkraut, prune—as well as a mock "Mr. Pierogi" contest and lawnmower parade. Despite being urban, the neighboring Indiana Dunes National Park provides RV camping among dunes and oak savannas.

Southwest USA

Albuquerque International Balloon Fiesta - Albuquerque, NM (early October).

Hundreds of hot air balloons flood the sky at dawn during this week-long visual extravaganza. RVers may reserve prime balloon field parking or choose adjacent campsites with shuttle service. On-site vendors provide Navajo fry bread, piñon coffee, and green chile cheeseburgers.

Texas Onion Festival - Weslaco, TX (late March)

The Rio Grande Valley will host blooming onion contests, salsa tastings, and onion cook-offs to commemorate the delicious Texas 1015 onion. The festival celebrates the region's agricultural legacy with live Tejano music and family activities. Local RV parks abound, with pull-through sites and citrus trees.

Rocky Mountains

Montana Folk Festival - Butte, Montana (mid-July)

This high-elevation city transforms into a cultural crossroads for three days of music, storytelling, and ethnic cuisine. Savor huckleberry delicacies, pasties, and indigenous bison recipes while watching free performances on numerous outdoor stages. Dry camping is accessible near the event grounds, with hookups at Thompson Park or the Fairmont RV Resort.

Colorado BBQ Challenge in Frisco, CO (mid-June)

Set against the Tenmile Range, this BBQ battle attracts pitmasters from all over the nation. After sampling the ribs, brisket, and pulled pork, take a walk around the beer garden or attend a whiskey lecture. The Frisco Peninsula Recreation Area offers RV camping with lake views, whilst Tiger Run RV Resort has luxurious facilities.

Pacific Northwest

Oregon Truffle Festival - Eugene, OR (late January - February)

This celebration of local truffles combines fine dining with foraging in the wild. Attend farm-to-table meals, cooking classes, and even truffle dog demonstrations. While winter temperatures might be moist, the adjacent Armitage Park RV Campground has year-round full-hookup sites and heated facilities.

Dungeness Crab & Seafood Festival in Port Angeles, Washington (mid-October)

Sample freshly caught crab, salmon chowder, and oyster shooters while watching renowned chefs perform gourmet demonstrations. This event, held on the Strait of Juan de Fuca, showcases seafood at its freshest and most picturesque. The fairgrounds allow dry camping, while Salt Creek Recreation Area has full-service sites and bluffside paths.

West Coast and California

Gilroy Garlic Festival - Gilroy, California (Late July)
Though the concept has changed in recent years, this iconic festival still honors the "stinking rose" with garlicky ice cream, pasta, and cookery contests. Check for updates on event locations and dates. Coyote Lake-Harvey Bear Ranch Park, located near downtown Gilroy, is a popular RV park.

Paso Robles Olive Festival - Paso Robles, California (mid-May)

Artisan oils, tapenades, and olive-laden foods are the highlights here, with local wines and music rounding out the experience. This event, held in California's Central Coast wine area, is a culinary feast. Wine Country RV Resort and Vines RV Resort both provide luxurious accommodations, including pools, tasting rooms, and shuttle service.

Alaska and Hawaii

Golden Days Festival - Fairbanks, Alaska (mid-July)

Celebrate Alaska's Gold Rush history with parades, riverside games, and sourdough pancake breakfasts. Expect midnight sun celebrations and gold panning competitions. RVers may find full hookups at River's Edge Resort and Pioneer Park Campground on the Chena River.

Kauai Coconut Festival - Kapaa, Hawaii (October).

For RVers brave enough to rent a campervan on the Garden Isle, this festival celebrates the coconut with hula, crafts, and coconut food ranging from curries to cream pies. Overnight camping licenses are available from Kauai County, however regulations and amenities vary.

Tips for Festival RVing

Book Early: Festival-adjacent campsites sometimes fill up months in advance, particularly for large events like the Balloon Fiesta or Tulip Time.

Boondocking savvy: Many events include dry camping in overflow areas or near fairgrounds. Bring leveling blocks, solar panels, and a lot of water.

Local Flavor: Avoid chain eateries. Festival food courts, mom-and-pop restaurants, and farm markets provide hyper-local taste and insight into regional character.

Pack accordingly: From foldable seats to walkie-talkies, a little planning may make packed festival conditions more pleasurable. Remember to bring cash for rural sellers and portable coolers for perishable items.

Consider the Altitude: Festivals may be held at altitudes higher than 6,000 feet, particularly in mountain regions. Hydrate, pace yourself, and monitor tire pressure and engine performance to make high-altitude changes.

Final Word:

These festivals are more than simply gatherings; they are seasonal milestones. Consider each meeting as a cultural stop during your 2025 RV journey: an opportunity to appreciate the tales, sounds, and aromas that distinguish each area as distinctly American.

Chapter 7: Campground & RV Park Directory

Top-Rated Campgrounds by Region

Choosing the perfect campsite may make or break your RV trip. This section has rigorously chosen, top-rated campsites around the United States, sorted by area for ease of planning. These campsites were assessed based on their accessibility, facilities, scenic value, closeness to attractions, and user happiness. Whether you desire wooded quiet, seaside pleasure, or full-service luxury, this regional guide has recommendations for every tourist.

Northeast

1. Normandy Farms Family Camping Resort, Foxborough, Massachusetts
Region: Southern New England

Highlights: Award-winning resort with full hookups, four pools, bike park, dog kennel, and wellness center.

Why Does It Stand Out: This campsite is immaculately maintained and family-friendly, combining rustic charm with resort-level conveniences. Ideal for anyone visiting Cape Cod or Boston.

Peak Season Tip: For summer weekends, make reservations far in advance.

2. Lake George RV Park at Lake George, New York, Adirondack region.

Highlights include 120+ acres, paved sites, trolley transportation, an aquatic park, and dog-friendly facilities.

Access: Close to I-87 and an ideal basecamp for Adirondack excursions.

Notable Nearby attractions include Lake George Village, hiking paths, and steamboat tours.

Southeast

1. Henderson Beach State Park in Destin, Florida Region: Florida Panhandle

Highlights include private beach access, nature walks, and well-shaded campsites.

Why Does It Stand Out: One of the few Gulf-front state parks with pure white sand beaches and dune ecosystems, providing a peaceful, uncrowded piece of coastal heaven.

Water and power (30/50 amp) hookups are available, as is an on-site waste station.

2. Anchor Down RV Resort, Dandridge, Tennessee Region: Great Smoky Mountains.

Highlights include lakefront sites, concrete pads, luxurious bathhouses, and golf cart rentals.

Ideal for those looking for mountain vistas and water sports, as well as convenient access to Pigeon Forge and the Great Smoky Mountains National Park.

Bonuses include fireplaces at premium sites and on-site food trucks during peak season.

Midwest

1. Door County KOA Holiday in Sturgeon Bay, Wisconsin Region: Great Lakes.

Highlights include wooded plots, access to wine regions, and a wide range of family facilities.

Signature Feature: Provides an ideal position for exploring the Door Peninsula's beaches, cherry orchards, and lighthouses.

RV-Friendly: Large rigs welcome, with luxurious patio sites available.

2. Sundermeier RV Park in St. Charles, Missouri Region: Midwest Heartland.

Highlights include paved full-hookup sites, historic Main Street within walking distance, and riverside walks.

Why It's Notable: A distinct combination of urban access and Mississippi River beauty, aimed toward RVers who value accessibility to eating, shopping, and culture.

Southwest

1. Dead Horse Ranch State Park, Cottonwood, Arizona Region: Verde Valley

Highlights include riverside camping, animal watching, hiking and bike routes.

Advantages include cool elevation and year-round comfort. A wonderful location for seeing Sedona and Jerome sans crowds.

Water and electric (30/50 amp), with a central waste station.

2. Sand Hollow State Park in Hurricane, Utah Region: Greater Zion.

Highlights: Beautiful red rock vistas, off-roading paths, and a warm-water reservoir.

Popular among adventure lovers who combine RVing with kayaking, UTVing, or cliff diving.

Insider Tip: Lakeside basic campsites fill up fast; prepare ahead of time to get the finest location.

West

1. Yosemite Pines RV Resort in Groveland, California Region: Sierra Nevada

Highlights: Full hookups, safari tents, petting zoo, and convenient access to Yosemite.

Why RVers love it: Combines resort-style amenities with wilderness access, making it perfect for RVers wishing to experience Yosemite without the crowds of in-park camping.

Proximity: around 22 miles from Yosemite's Big Oak Flat entrance.

2. Silver Spur RV Park, Silverton, Oregon Region: Willamette Valley

Highlights include immaculately groomed gardens, wine country access, and event space.

Special Features: Clubhouse, hot tub, and walking paths. A classy alternative in an area abounding with wine and waterfalls.

Pacific Northwest

1. Cape Disappointment State Park in Ilwaco, Washington Region: Pacific Coast

Highlights include oceanfront camping, spectacular cliffs, and ancient lighthouses.

Atmosphere: Moody coastal scenery with miles of paths and interpretative centers.

Important Information: Reserve early; beachfront plots are in great demand.

2. Sun outside. Coos Bay is located on the southern Oregon coast.

Highlights include spacious full-hookup campsites, beach access, and scheduled activities.

Why Visit: It combines isolated seaside beauty with contemporary comfort. Whale viewing and tide-pooling are only steps away from your campsite.

Rocky Mountains

1. Tiger Run Resort in Breckenridge, Colorado Region: Central Rockies

Highlights: Luxury resort with a clubhouse, indoor pool, and breathtaking mountain views.

Winter-Ready: Open year-round, with heated water lines—ideal for winter visitors.

Ideal Location: Close to Breckenridge and the Tenmile Range for hiking, biking, or skiing.

2. Colter Bay RV Park in the Jackson Hole region of Grand Teton National Park, Wyoming

Highlights include forested sites, marina access, and breathtaking views of the Tetons.

Standout feature: It is located within the park, providing easy access to animals and trails in the mornings.

Hookups: Full sewer service, which is unusual for a national park campsite.

Alaska

1. Seward Waterfront Park in Seward, Alaska (Kenai Peninsula)

Highlights include views of the glacial fjord, harbor-front camping, and a short stroll to downtown Seward.

Best for: Those want to see Alaska's spectacular vistas without compromising convenience.

Open season: May to September. Water and electricity are provided, with waste stations closed.

2. Denali Rainbow Village RV Park in Denali National Park, Alaska. Region: Interior Alaska

Highlights: Beautiful riverside location, easy park shuttle access, and nearby amenities.

In Demand: Serves as an excellent basecamp for people looking for full-day trips into Denali.

Navigation Tips for Selecting Campgrounds

Reservation Systems: Many high-quality campsites utilize ReserveAmerica, Recreation.gov, or direct booking via independent websites. Always verify the cancellation policies.

Connectivity is Important: Not all campsites have mobile signals or Wi-Fi. Use coverage maps or offline applications to prepare ahead.

Stay Duration: High-demand locations often impose stay limitations. Consider using surrounding public lands or private RV parks for overflow or prolonged stays.

connection Clarity: A "full hookup" often includes water, sewage, and 30/50 amp electricity. Always double-check details, particularly in state or national parks.

Off-Season Gems: Some of the best campsites shine brightest during the shoulder seasons—fall in the Northeast, spring in the Southwest, and late summer in the Rockies.

This area roundup provides a good basis for creating a memorable RV adventure. Each of the campgrounds featured is more than just a place to park; it is a destination in its own right. Use this map to connect picturesque, peaceful, and well-equipped accommodations for a more efficient road trip in 2025.

Public vs. Private Parks

The United States has a huge and diversified network of RV-friendly campgrounds, each fulfilling a distinct role in the larger travel ecology. RVers traveling across the nation in 2025 will meet both public and private campsites, and recognizing the distinctions is critical for planning efficient, fun, and cost-effective itineraries.

Public Parks: Federal and State Managed Lands

Public parks in the United States are controlled at many government levels, including federal, state, county, and municipal. These properties are protected for leisure, conservation, and public pleasure, giving RV travelers access to some of the country's most beautiful landscapes.

1. National parks.

These are America's crown jewels and are managed by the National Park Service (NPS). From Yellowstone's geysers to Yosemite's granite cliffs, national parks provide unparalleled natural beauty and famous views. However, not all are suitable for RVers. Common limits include limited campground availability, vehicle length restrictions (typically between 27 and 35 feet), and a lack of full connections.

Reservations are required months in advance, particularly during high seasons.

Amenities are often minimal, with dry camping, trash stations, and rudimentary bathrooms.

Cost: Affordable ($20-$35 per night), with savings available via the America the Beautiful Pass and Senior/Access passes.

Ideal for: scenic immersion, hiking, animal observation, and photography.

2. National Forest and BLM Lands
Managed by the U.S. Forest Service and Bureau of Land Management, these areas are RV-friendly havens for visitors seeking independence and isolation. While constructed campsites exist, scattered camping (boondocking) is often allowed for free and with minimal restrictions.

Reservations are often not necessary; first-come, first-served is normal.

Amenities: primitive to semi-developed; generators are often allowed.

Cost ranges from free to $20 each night.

Best for off-grid camping, extended stays, and distant exploring.

3. State parks
Each state administers its own network of parks, frequently exhibiting regional ecosystems and historical landmarks. State parks tend to provide well-maintained amenities, paved sites, and picturesque surroundings.

Reservations are common and often made via state park portals.

Amenities vary greatly; many have power and water connections, dump stations, and bathhouses.

Cost: Midrange ($25-$50 per night), with out-of-state surcharges in some areas.

Ideal for: Family camping, outdoor activities, and scheduled trips.

4. Regional, County, and Municipal Parks.

These neighborhood parks are sometimes neglected jewels. They are often located near small towns or picturesque corridors and provide a quieter alternative to major locations, with less tourists.

Reservations vary by location.

Amenities: May include hookups, Wi-Fi, playgrounds, and picnic spaces.

Cost-effective ($10-$35 each night).

Ideal for: Short stays, peaceful settings, and community involvement.

Private parks provide commercial comfort and convenience.

Private RV parks are run by corporations or people and often provide more contemporary amenities and constant service. They are located near roads, attractions, and metropolitan areas and serve both overnight travelers and long-term residents.

1. Chain campgrounds (such as KOA, Good Sam, and Yogi Bear's Jellystone Park).
Well-known brands provide reliability and conveniences on the road. These campgrounds are ideal for families and full-timers seeking convenience.

Reservations are recommended and frequently bookable via app or website.

Amenities include full hookups, Wi-Fi, laundry, pools, playgrounds, and event programming.

Cost: Moderate to premium ($40–$90/night), with loyalty program discounts.

Best For: Family travels, destination stops, and creature comforts.

2. Independent RV Parks.
These parks vary from low-cost mom-and-pop businesses to posh resorts with clubhouses and concierge services. Quality varies, but many have a local charm that chains cannot match.

Reservations: Usually available; call ahead or check campground apps.

Amenities often include complete hookups, cable TV, Wi-Fi, toilets, and pet spaces.

Costs vary from $25 to $100 or more each night, depending on location and facilities.

Best for: Flexible routes, long stays, and a social atmosphere.

3. RV Resorts and 55+ Communities. RV resorts are designed for seasonal snowbirds and retirees, providing upscale, resort-style living with a strong sense of community. Gated access, exercise facilities, golf, and social activities are commonplace.

Reservations: Often necessary months ahead during heavy season.

Premium amenities include full hookups, high-speed internet, clubhouses, pools, and more.

Cost: High-end ($60-$150+/night); weekly and monthly rates available.

Ideal for: Long-term stays, winter getaways, and active adult lives.

Choosing What Is Right for Your Journey

The appropriate balance depends on the sort of vacation. For visual immersion and affordability, public parks are unparalleled. For stability, convenience, and access to full-service facilities, private parks win. Many experienced RVers combine the two, boondocking in a national forest one week and plugging into a full-hookup resort the next.

Whether you're chasing waterfalls in the Pacific Northwest or driving Route 66 through the heartland, understanding the park landscape will help you plan your trip, improve your comfort, and enrich your experience.

Insider Tip: Use applications like Campendium, RV LIFE Trip Wizard, and the Dyrt Pro to get real-time ratings, site availability, and GPS-friendly planning for both public and private campgrounds.

Hookup Availability & Amenities

Navigating the complexities of campground services is as important to RV travel as having gasoline in the tank. Whether you're boondocking in the desert or staying at a luxury RV park, knowing what to anticipate in terms of hookups and facilities may have a big impact on your schedule, daily routine, and overall comfort. This section delves into the major factors of connection availability and campground amenities, providing visitors with the information they need to plan properly, avoid surprises, and make the most of each trip.

Types of RV hookups

Full hookups

A full hookup site often provides power, water, and sewage. These sites provide the maximum degree of convenience, allowing for extended stays without the need to relocate the car to empty tanks or replenish water. Full connections are typical in many private RV parks, state parks with contemporary infrastructure, and bigger campsites around the nation.

Electricity is most often provided in 30- and 50-amp forms. Newer RVs including those with twin air conditioners often demand 50 amps.

Water: Potable, pressured water for shipboard consumption.

Sewer: Direct drainage from the RV's waste system, which eliminates the need for repeated excursions to the dump station.

Partial connections

These properties often have power and water, but no sewage hookup. They are prevalent in national parks, older campsites, and picturesque regions with minimal infrastructure. Partial connections are ideal for short stays or RVs with bigger holding tanks.

Electric-Only Sites

Electric-only sites, which are available on certain public lands and in remote areas, give basic electricity but require RVers to save water and prepare for dumping at central stations. These are great for those who want a mix of comfort and seclusion.

Dry camping / No hookups

This kind of camping, sometimes known as "boondocking," includes no direct connections. It requires self-sufficiency, depending on onboard water storage, battery systems, and waste tanks. This kind of camping is often free or inexpensive, and it appeals to individuals seeking isolation, scenic beauty, or a stronger connection with nature.

Utility Connections: Expect Power Pedestals.

Most established RV parks include pedestal units at each campground. They often include:

20-, 30-, and 50-amp outlets

Circuit breakers

Nighttime Lighting

Occasionally, coaxial or fiber-optic cable connections (in luxury parks).

Water Spigots.

Standard hose bibbs deliver drinkable water, however the pressure might fluctuate. A pressure regulator is suggested to safeguard the onboard plumbing.

Sewer Connections

Sewer inlets are ground-level and may be threaded or open. Use a secure sewage hose connection with a suitable seal to prevent spills or contamination.

Campground Amenities: Beyond the Basics.

Modern RV campsites vary from basic clearings to full-service resorts with a variety of amenities. Here's a list of common and premium amenities found in the United States:

Amenities

Dump Stations are designated sites for emptying gray and black tanks, often free for visitors and accessible for a modest price for passerby.

Bathhouses and laundromats are useful for saving water or accommodating bigger crowds. Cleanliness and availability vary depending on locale.

Wi-Fi and Cell Boosters Available in many RV sites, however bandwidth may be restricted during busy hours.

Rural areas often lack signal strength; some provide mobile signal boosters or satellite-based internet.

Clubhouses and Recreation Areas - These are common at bigger resorts and may feature kitchens, lounges, pools, hot tubs, workout rooms, or planned social activities.

Pet-friendly areas include dog parks, washing facilities, and off-leash zones for RV travelers.

Propane fill stations provide handy on-site refill alternatives for cooking, heating, and refrigeration.

Security and Gated Access - Premium parks may have 24-hour personnel, gated entrances, and monitoring for added peace of mind.

Onsite Maintenance: Some sites provide mobile repair services and on-call personnel for minor difficulties.

Long-term parks may include mail forwarding, faxing, and printing services for full-time and distant workers.

Seasonal considerations

Some amenities are not accessible year-round. Water lines and disposal stations in colder climates may shut or be restricted during the winter months. Campground fees and service availability sometimes change depending on the season and occupancy.

Key Symbols on RV Maps

This atlas employs a standard collection of symbols to represent connection kinds and significant features. Refer to the legend for simple identification while planning routes. For example:

⚡ - Electric connection (amp rating)

💧 - Water connection

🚽 - Sewer hookup

👕: Laundry facilities

▪ Wi-Fi is accessible.

🐾: Pet area

🔒 - Gated/security access.

🌊 - Pool/spa

Pro Tip for Maximizing Utility Access: Reserve Early: Full hookup sites are in high demand, particularly at popular parks and during peak travel seasons.

Carry converters: Give your RV 30-to-50 amp converters and extension cables for versatility in various locations.

Use a Surge Protector to protect your RV's electrical system from unreliable campground power sources.

Tank Conservation: When staying at partial or dry sites, keep check of tank levels on a regular basis to prevent surprises.

Plan Dumps Strategically: Before staying at no-sewer locations, find out where the nearest dump stations are.

Understanding hookup availability and campground amenities enables RVers to choose destinations that fit their lifestyle, gear, and travel rhythm. Whether you choose rural serenity or resort-level amenities, the correct configuration guarantees easier, smarter travel in 2025 and beyond.

Booking Resources & Membership Clubs

Planning a smooth RV drive across the United States in 2025 requires more than just knowing the routes; it also needs the correct connections. Booking resources and membership clubs are the silent motors that drive efficient travel, providing significant discounts, access to special campsites, and a more seamless overall experience. This section serves as your strategic command center, providing an in-depth overview of the platforms, initiatives, and relationships that wise RVers depend on.

Top Online Booking Platforms.

1. Campendium.

Campendium is ideal for boondockers and RVers looking for diversity, since it provides user-generated evaluations of over 30,000 public and private camping places. Cell signal strength, facilities, elevation, and nightly pricing are among the search options available. The platform works perfectly with GPS tools, and the premium edition provides cell coverage maps and trail access.

2. RV Life (Trip Wizard).

This site is great for planning as well as booking. Enter your rig's dimensions to avoid low clearances and restricted highways. Connect it to the RV Life app for GPS-based turn-by-turn navigation. Users may book campsites directly or via links to official campground websites.

3. The Dyrt Pro

The Dyrt PRO's data-rich UI and offline map access make it perfect for distant travel. Members have access to Dyrt Alerts, which warn you when cancellations become available at fully booked campsites. The program also allows you to book at thousands of paid and free places, including BLM and national forests.

4. Recreation.gov

This is the straight pipeline for those who like visiting national parks. Reserve campsites, purchase permits, and arrange timed entrance tickets to popular parks such as Yosemite and Glacier. The absence of intermediaries is a significant benefit. This is a must-have digital toolset for RVers looking to explore natural beauty.

5. Harvest Hosts and Boondockers. Welcome

Not a standard booking service, but a membership-based network that provides unique overnight stays in wineries, farms, museums, and other destinations. Book using an app, contact your host, and enjoy dry camping in picturesque, off-grid areas with local culture.

Essential Membership Clubs for RV Travel

1. Good Sam Club.

A long-standing member of the RVing community. Members get:

10% off at more than 2,000 partner campsites.

Fuel savings at several Pilot Flying J stations.

Roadside assistance options

Discounts for RV parts and accessories

The annual cost is reasonable, and the advantages often outweigh the charge within a few nights.

2. Passport America.

Known for offering considerable campsite discounts of up to 50%. Is there a catch? Restrictions on peak seasons and stay duration. Long-term stays should be avoided in favour of off-season or en route stopovers. It immediately pays for itself after just a few usage.

3. Escapees RV Club offers social support and practical assistance. Members have access to:

Discounted camping via the SKP Co-op network

RV education: webinars and bootcamps

Mail forwarding services for full-time

Advocacy for RVers' Rights

Escapees also organize huge rallies and local neighborhood meetings around the country.

4. Family Motor Coach Association (FMCA)
Not only for families; available to all motorhome and towable RV owners. Benefits include:

FMCAssist provides emergency medical evacuation coverage.

Exclusive RV insurance policies.

Tire discount schemes with major brands.

Access to member-only campsites and rally activities.

FMCA offers safety, savings, and friendship in a close-knit network.

5. Thousand Trails.
Thousand Trails is a game changer for RVers who want to stay in resort-style campsites for extended periods. Members pay a set charge for admission to campsites within a certain zone. Add-ons broaden your options or provide more sophisticated booking periods. Pools, clubhouses, and activity calendars are among the expected features.

6. KOA Rewards.
The Kampgrounds of America network includes a variety of settings, ranging from rustic to resort-level. KOA Rewards members will receive:

10% nightly discount.

Points to future stays

Early information about site availability and discounts.

It's a simple, user-friendly software for individuals who are devoted to a well-known brand.

Specialty and Regional Clubs to Consider: Happy Camper Club. Offers a 50% discount at independent campsites around the country. Although it has a smaller area than Passport America, the premise is identical. Ideally used in combination with other clubs.

Harvest Hosts + Golf Upgrade - Includes private golf courses and country clubs among your overnight selections. This is a one-of-a-kind benefit for people traveling with clubs.

State Park Passes - Some states (such as Texas, California, and Colorado) provide yearly passes that waive admission and camping costs. These may result in significant savings over time.

To maximize value, consider layering your memberships. Use Passport America or Good Sam for overnight stays, and Thousand Trails or Escapees for longer stays. Stack memberships to suit your travel preferences.

Book Early in Peak Season: National and state park campsites often accept reservations 6 months in advance. Set reminders and reserve the locations when they become available.

Use Alerts and Cancellation Trackers: Tools like Campnab or Dyrt PRO's Cancellations Alerts may help you get good slots even when your schedule is filled.

Know Your Rig's Specifications: Use the RV Life Trip Wizard to avoid small roads, low bridges, and dead ends. Booking a gorgeous spot is nothing if you can't get there securely.

Final Word

The wide road benefits the prepared. The most effective itineraries begin with a plan rather than a map. Booking systems provide accuracy. Membership groups provide value. Together, they make a decent RV vacation into an amazing one. Align your tools, understand your networks, and let these resources take you into the heart of America, one campground at a time.

Chapter 8: Maps & Route Overviews

State-by-State RV Road Maps

Navigating the vast and diverse landscapes of the United States requires more than just a GPS. It takes a systematic approach to route design that combines efficiency, scenic beauty, and local character. This section provides a comprehensive state-by-state overview, highlighting significant RV-friendly roads, backroad options, important milestones, and interesting diversions to enhance each route.

Alabama's key routes include Interstate 65 (I-65), which connects Mobile in the south to Birmingham and then to Tennessee. For coastal tourists, U.S. Highway 98 follows the Gulf coast, providing sweeping ocean vistas and access to gorgeous beaches.

Scenic Alternatives: The Natchez Trace Parkway, a historic 444-mile road across Alabama, provides a peaceful, car-free environment suited for RVs looking for a leisurely trip rich in history and wildlife.

RV-Friendly Stops: Visit Gulf State Park's best campsite in Gulf Shores or the shaded sites at Cheaha State Park, which sits on Alabama's highest point.

Alaska's main route for RVers is the Alaska Highway, which spans 1,390 miles from Dawson Creek. Within Alaska, the Parks Highway links Anchorage and Fairbanks, passing via Denali National Park.

Navigation Tips: Fuel and services might be scarce. Careful preparation with comprehensive maps is essential, particularly when traversing isolated areas such as the Dalton Highway.

Scenic Highlights: For an unforgettable wilderness experience, take a diversion down the Seward Highway, known for its fjords and animals, or follow the Glenn Highway through alpine panoramas.

Arizona's key routes include Interstate 40, which connects historic Route 66 cities like Kingman and Flagstaff. Interstate 17 links Phoenix and Flagstaff, passing through wooded mountain scenery.

Scenic Alternatives: The Apache Trail (State Route 88) snakes through the Superstition Mountains, providing a rocky, panoramic journey ideal for compact RVs or trailers.

RV Parks and Stops: Enjoy facilities at Lake Pleasant Regional Park in Phoenix or the huge desert campgrounds that encircle Tucson.

Arkansas has two key routes: Interstate 40 connects Little Rock to Fort Smith and beyond, while Interstate 30 connects Little Rock to Texarkana and Texas.

Scenic Routes: The Ozark National Forest has a network of backroads and byways that lead to spring-fed rivers, bluffs, and hiking trails—ideal for RVers looking for nature without crowds.

Recommended stops: The Buffalo National River region offers rustic campsites and lovely river drives.

California Key Routes: The famed Pacific Coast Highway (State Route 1) offers breathtaking coastal vistas from Orange County to the northern border. Interstate 5 is a quick north-south road that connects large metropolitan areas such as Los Angeles, Sacramento, and Portland, Oregon.

Scenic Routes: The Sierra Nevada's Tioga Pass (Highway 120) runs through Yosemite National Park and is a must-see in the summer.

RV Parks & Facilities: California has a wide range of RV camping options, including large campsites in Joshua Tree National Park and beachside parks in Santa Barbara.

Colorado's key routes include Interstate 70, which runs east-west across the Rockies and passes via Denver, Vail, and Aspen ski resorts. U.S. Highway 550, known as the "Million Dollar Highway," is a thrilling, tight mountain drive with steep cliffs and panoramic vistas.

Scenic Backroads: Trail Ridge Road in Rocky Mountain National Park, which is accessible seasonally, ascends to almost 12,000 feet and is ideal for RV travelers seeking high-altitude views.

RV Stops: Several state parks, including Cherry Creek and Golden Gate Canyon, provide well-maintained RV facilities.

Connecticut's key routes include Interstate 95, which connects New York City to Rhode Island, and Interstate 84, which connects Danbury and Hartford.

picturesque Routes: The Merritt Parkway is a historic, picturesque highway known for its antique bridges and lush canopy, but it does not allow big vehicles; verify RV size before planning.

RV Friendly Areas: Campgrounds along the Connecticut River and state parks such as Hammonasset Beach provide easy coastline access.

Delaware's primary routes are Interstate 95 and U.S. Route 13, which connect the northern and southern coastal regions.

Route 9 meanders through Delaware's maritime woodlands and bayside villages, providing a calmer option for RVs wanting a seaside ambiance.

Recommended Camping: Cape Henlopen State Park, near Lewes, has well-maintained RV sites with handy beach access.

Key routes in Florida include Interstate 95 and 75, which run north-south along the east and west coasts, respectively. The Florida Turnpike is a toll road that connects central and southern Florida.

Scenic Routes: The Overseas Highway (US 1) runs across the Florida Keys, connecting Key Largo and Key West via hundreds of bridges and blue waters—essential for any RV road trip.

RV Facilities: Florida has several RV resorts, ranging from seaside sites in Fort Lauderdale to campgrounds in Everglades National Park.

Georgia's key routes include Interstate 75, which connects Atlanta to the Florida border. Interstate 20 runs east to west, linking Atlanta to Augusta and South Carolina.

beautiful Drives: The Russell-Brasstown Scenic Byway in the North Georgia Mountains passes through deep woods and waterfalls, ideal for leisurely, beautiful RV driving.

Camping: The Chattahoochee National Forest has many RV-friendly campsites with mountain views.

Hawaii

Travel Note: Due to Hawaii's island layout, RV travel is confined to certain islands where rental RVs are available. Roads are often small and twisting, requiring careful navigation.

Popular Routes: The Hana Highway on Maui is one of the most well-known beautiful drives, including waterfalls and coastline vistas along a small, twisting route.

RV Stops: On Oahu, campgrounds like Bellows Field Beach Park provide coastal sites.

Idaho's key routes include Interstate 84, which connects Boise to Oregon. U.S. Highway 93 north of Twin Falls provides spectacular views of the river canyon.

Scenic Routes: The Sawtooth Scenic Byway has breathtaking mountain scenery and alpine lakes.

RV Camping: Many state parks and national forests provide plenty of chances for wilderness camping with complete RV amenities.

Illinois' key routes include Interstate 55, which follows Route 66 from Chicago to St. Louis. Interstate 90 travels east-west throughout northern Illinois.

Scenic Options: The Great River Road along the Mississippi River is a lovely option for RVers seeking river vistas and small-town charm.

RV Parks: Campgrounds along the Illinois River and in Chicago's suburbs provide easy urban-rural transitions.

Interstate 65 travels north-south through Indianapolis. Interstate 70 links the western border with Ohio.

Scenic Drives: The Ohio River Scenic Byway in southern Indiana has undulating hills and historic river villages.

Brown County State Park provides spacious RV campsites among wooded hills.

Iowa's principal business and recreational route is Interstate 80, which runs from east to west.

Scenic Routes: The Loess Hills National Scenic Byway in western Iowa has unusual geological formations and vistas.

RV Facilities: Iowa's numerous state parks provide modern RV campsites among natural features.

Kansas' key routes include Interstate 70, which connects Kansas City and Denver.

Scenic Drives: The Flint Hills National Scenic Byway displays unique and magnificent tallgrass prairie scenery.

Camping: Tallgrass grassland National Preserve provides RV camping in a grassland habitat.

Kentucky's key routes include Interstate 75 connecting the northern section to Tennessee and Interstate 64 running east-west throughout the state.

The Red River Gorge Scenic Byway in the Daniel Boone National Forest has breathtaking natural bridges and rock formations.

RV Stops: Cumberland Falls State Resort Park has RV sites beside one of the state's most spectacular waterfalls.

Interstate 10 connects New Orleans with Baton Rouge, crossing Louisiana from east to west.

gorgeous Options: The Great River Road along the Mississippi River has historic and cultural sites as well as gorgeous river vistas.

Camping: Bayou State Park provides bayou-side camping experiences.

Maine's key routes include Interstate 95, which connects Portland and Bangor.

Scenic Drives: Coastal Route 1 follows the craggy coastline, past gorgeous lighthouses, fishing communities, and rocky beaches.

RV Facilities: Many state parks along the coast provide beachside camping.

Maryland's key routes include Interstate 95, which passes through Baltimore and near Washington, DC.

Scenic Routes: The Chesapeake Country Scenic Byway travels through historic communities and rivers along the Chesapeake Bay.

Camping: Assateague State Park provides coastal camping with wild ponies nearby.

Massachusetts' key routes include Interstate 90 (Mass Pike), which connects Boston to the western border.

Scenic drives include Route 6A along Cape Cod, which has attractive coastal communities and beaches.

RV Stops: The Cape Cod National Seashore offers campsites with views of the dunes and the ocean.

Michigan's key routes include Interstate 75, which connects Detroit to the Upper Peninsula.

Scenic Drives: The Tunnel of Trees on M-119 near Lake Michigan features forest-lined roads with lake views.

RV Facilities: Several state parks around the Great Lakes have well-equipped campsites.

Minnesota's key routes include Interstate 35, which connects the Twin Cities and Duluth.

Scenic Routes: The North Shore Scenic Drive along Lake Superior is popular for its panoramic views of the lake and forest.

Camping: The Superior National Forest and Boundary Waters Canoe Area provide remote RV camping.

Mississippi's main route is Interstate 55, which runs north-south through its heart.

Scenic Routes: The Natchez Trace Parkway extends into Mississippi, providing historic attractions and tranquil scenery.

RV Parks: Several state parks have shaded camping beside rivers.

Missouri's key routes include Interstate 70, which connects Kansas City and St. Louis.

The Ozark Scenic Byway has undulating hills, beautiful rivers, and caverns.

Camping: The Mark Twain National Forest has several RV sites in wooded regions.

Montana's key routes include Interstate 90, which runs across the state's south.

Scenic Drives: The Going-to-the-Sun Road via Glacier National Park is famed for its alpine splendor.

RV Camping: Many national and state parks provide camping at high altitudes and in wilderness areas.

Nebraska's key routes include Interstate 80, which runs east-west.

Scenic Routes: The Sandhills Journey. Scenic Byway has one of North America's greatest sand dune formations.

Camping: State parks provide amenities near lakes and rivers.

Nevada's key routes include Interstate 15, which links Las Vegas to Salt Lake City.

Route 50, "The Loneliest Road," crosses the desert with few stops but spectacular mountain views.

RV campgrounds: There are several campgrounds around Las Vegas and Lake Tahoe that cater to RV tourists.

New Hampshire's key routes include Interstate 93, which connects Massachusetts and the White Mountains.

Scenic Drives: The Kancamagus Highway provides spectacular mountain and woodland vistas.

campsites: The White Mountain National Forest has substantial RV campsites.

Key routes in New Jersey include Interstate 95 (New Jersey Turnpike), which runs north-south.

Scenic routes include the Delaware River Scenic Byway, which offers river vistas and historic villages.

RV Camping: State parks along the Jersey Shore provide seaside camping.

Key routes in New Mexico include Interstate 40, which travels east-west, and Interstate 25, which goes north-south.

picturesque Routes: The Turquoise Trail links Albuquerque and Santa Fe with mining communities and picturesque views.

RV Stops: Campgrounds near Carlsbad Caverns and the Rio Grande Gorge provide good amenities.

New York's key routes include Interstate 90, which connects Buffalo and Albany.

Scenic routes include the Adirondack Trail, which runs across the Adirondack Mountains and offers vistas of lakes and forests.

RV Facilities: There are several state parks and campsites across the state, including those near Niagara Falls.

North Carolina's key routes are Interstate 85, which links Charlotte to Durham, and Interstate 40, which travels east-west.

Scenic Routes: The Blue Ridge Parkway passes across the western highlands, providing breathtaking views.

RV Camping: Great Smoky Mountains National Park has many RV-friendly campsites.

North Dakota's key routes include Interstate 94, which connects Fargo and Bismarck.

Scenic Routes: The Enchanted Highway is a rural byway lined with enormous metal sculptures.

Camping: Theodore Roosevelt National Park has both rustic and sophisticated campgrounds.

Ohio
Key Routes: Interstates 70 and 71 link major cities across Ohio.

Scenic Routes: The Ohio River Scenic Byway runs through southern river communities.

RV Parks: Several state parks provide handy camping alternatives.

Oklahoma's key routes are Interstate 35, which runs north-south, and Interstate 40, which travels east-west.

Scenic Routes: The Talimena Scenic Drive winds across the Ouachita Mountains, affording wooded views.

Camping: Lake Murray State Park has numerous RV sites.

Oregon's key routes include Interstate 5, which runs north-south, and U.S. Highway 101, which follows the coast.

Scenic Drives: The Oregon Coast Scenic Byway is known for its cliffs, beaches, and lighthouses.

RV Stops: Several state parks provide coastal camping.

In Pennsylvania, Interstate 80 runs east-west and Interstate 81 travels north-south. These are the key routes.

Scenic Routes: The Laurel Highlands Scenic Byway has hilly woodland vistas.

Camping: RV travelers may stay at state parks near the Pocono Mountains.

Key routes in Rhode Island include Interstate 95, which runs across the state.

Ocean Drive in Newport provides beach vistas and houses.

Camping: State parks include tiny campsites along the sea.

South Carolina's key routes include Interstate 95, which runs north-south, and Interstate 26, which runs diagonally.

Scenic Route: The Cherokee Foothills Scenic Highway runs across the northwest slopes.

RV Parks: Campgrounds in Myrtle Beach and Charleston provide beach access.

South Dakota's key routes include Interstate 90, which runs east-west.

Scenic Routes: The Peter Norbeck Scenic Byway encircles Mount Rushmore with spectacular rock formations.

Camping: Black Hills National Forest includes various RV sites.

Tennessee Key Routes: Interstate 40 spans east-west between Nashville and Knoxville.

Scenic Routes: The Cherohala Skyway is a mountain byway offering panoramic views.

RV Facilities: The Great Smoky Mountains National Park has substantial RV campsites.

Texas has two key routes: Interstate 35 goes north-south and Interstate 10 travels east-west.

Scenic Routes: The Hill Country Scenic Byway in central Texas has undulating hills and wildflowers.

Camping: State parks such as Garner and Lost Maples provide great RV campsites.

Utah's key routes are Interstate 15 (north-south) and Interstate 70 (east-west).

Scenic Byway 12 passes through red sandstone canyons and woodlands.

RV Stops: There are several campsites around Zion and Bryce Canyon National Parks.

Vermont's key routes are Interstate 89, which travels north-south, and Route 100, which provides picturesque rural vistas.

Scenic Drives: The Northeast Kingdom offers calm, wooded roads.

State parks and forest campsites welcome RV visitors.

Virginia Key Routes: Interstate 95 travels north-south along the eastern corridor.

Scenic Routes: Skyline Drive in Shenandoah National Park is known for autumn colors and vistas.

RV Facilities: Numerous campsites around the Blue Ridge Mountains.

Key routes in Washington include Interstate 5, which runs north-south.

Scenic Routes: The Cascade Loop Scenic Byway passes through mountains and lakes.

Camping: Mount Rainier and Olympic National Parks include a variety of RV campsites.

Key routes in West Virginia include Interstate 79, which travels north-south, and Interstate 64, which goes east-west.

Highland Scenic Highway provides rugged mountain vistas.

Camping: Multiple state parks and forests have RV facilities.

Wisconsin's key routes include Interstate 94, which runs east-west.

Scenic Routes: The Great River Road runs along the Mississippi River.

RV Stops: There are several state parks and lakefront campsites available.

Wyoming's main routes are Interstate 80, which travels east-west, and U.S. Highway 89, which goes north-south.

Scenic Routes: The Grand Teton National Park scenic roads provide views of towering peaks and animals.

Camping: Yellowstone National Park has various RV parks, but reservations are required.

This state-by-state overview provides RV travelers with important navigational tips, route options, and camping highlights. Routes may be tailored to individual preferences, from coastal drives and mountain passes to historic byways and desolate wilderness, ensuring a smarter, richer driving experience in 2025.

Fuel Station & Dump Site Locator

Navigating America's extensive network of roads and byways in an RV takes more than just a good map; it also necessitates accurate knowledge of where to refuel and handle garbage correctly. The "USA RVers Road Atlas 2025"'s Fuel Station & Dump Site Locator section is a must-have tool for making any RV travel easy, efficient, and environmentally responsible.

Fuel Stations: Finding Power for Your Journey

Fuel availability varies greatly according to the geography and kind of fuel used. Diesel remains the most popular fuel type for recreational vehicles, however many motorhomes still run on gasoline. The atlas focuses on a comprehensive network of petrol stations around the nation, with specific emphasis to:

Diesel pumps and DEF (Diesel Exhaust Fluid): Most current diesel RVs need DEF in addition to diesel fuel. Stations that provide DEF are conspicuously signposted, particularly along major interstate arteries and in outlying areas where services are rare.

24/7 Accessibility: Some gasoline stations provide round-the-clock service to RV travelers, which is especially important for lengthy trips or unexpected late arrivals. These stations are prioritized on the map and organized by state.

Large pump bays and easy maneuverability: Not all gasoline stations can easily handle an RV's length and height. The Atlas highlights stations with large, well-lit bays and simple ingress/egress to reduce the danger of damage or congestion.

Fuel Price Trends and Discounts: While prices fluctuate, some chains consistently provide competitive pricing or loyalty rewards to RV travelers. The appendix contains tips for using mobile applications and loyalty programs to save money now.

Alternative Fuel Options: Where appropriate, places providing propane refills, compressed natural gas (CNG), or electric charging stations for hybrid and electric RVs are highlighted for the environmentally concerned RV community.

Dump Sites: Responsible Waste Management.
Wastewater and solid waste disposal must be safe and lawful in order to protect human health, the environment, and comply with rules. This atlas section lists:

Public dump stations, which are located at strategic intervals along main highways, campsites, and rest places, often offer free or low-cost garbage disposal services. Each station is assessed based on its accessibility, hours of operation, and compatibility with different RV waste systems.

Private campsites and RV Parks: Many campsites include dump stations reserved solely for registered visitors, as well as facilities like drinkable water refill stations and chemical waste disposal. To prevent surprises, this map can help you plan stops near campsites that provide these amenities.

24-Hour Dump Facilities: For travelers with unpredictable schedules, having dump facilities available at all hours may be a lifesaver. These are particularly noticeable, usually around important transportation routes or metropolitan areas.

Environmental Compliance Tips: The document discusses proper trash disposal procedures, stressing the significance of utilizing designated dump sites to preserve groundwater and wildlife. It also includes similar regional norms and limits to help avoid penalties and environmental damage.

Portable Waste Management Solutions: For distant or boondocking circumstances, the atlas describes portable waste tank alternatives and provides guidance on when and where to securely empty them.

Integrated Fuel and Dump Stops for Optimal Routing
The atlas includes integrated location maps of gasoline stations and waste sites for strategic planning. These maps help you build routes that minimize needless diversions,

preserve gasoline, and enhance convenience. They factor in:

Distance Intervals: Typical RV fuel tank ranges and black/gray water capacity are used to determine optimum stop intervals.

Service Clusters: Highlighting clusters of several services lets RVers to refuel, discharge garbage, and relax all at one stop, increasing efficiency and lowering travel stress.

Emergency Stops: Locations designated for emergency fuel and garbage disposal are dispersed along rural roadways, which are critical for long-distance travelers passing through sparsely inhabited regions.

This portion of the atlas is regularly updated with information acquired from government transportation agencies, major fuel chains, RV clubs, and traveler reports to ensure accuracy and usefulness. When combined with the route maps and planning tools included elsewhere in this atlas, the Fuel Station & Dump Site Locator becomes an essential component of any successful RV excursion, making every mile profitable and every stop meaningful.

Made in the USA
Coppell, TX
04 June 2025

50301561R10142